Diepsloot

To Harriet, Jesse, Georgia and Zara –
whose support was unwavering.

Diepsloot

Anton Harber

Jonathan Ball Publishers
JOHANNESBURG & CAPE TOWN

Published in trade paperback in 2011 by
JONATHAN BALL PUBLISHERS (PTY) LTD
PO Box 33977
Jeppestown
2043

ISBN 978-1-86842-421-4

Reprinted twice in 2011
Reprinted once in 2012

Edited by Frances Perryer
Cover design by Michiel Botha
Text design by Triple M Design, Johannesburg
Set in 10.75/15.5 pt Sabon LT Std
Printed and bound by CTP Book Printers, Cape

Contents

By the side of the road, a place of fear

Drive north from Johannesburg along William Nicol Highway and you pass the glittering shopping malls of Hyde Park, Sandton and Fourways, and the faux-Italian casino playground called Montecasino. As you move further out of the city, you will be struck by the number and newness of gated communities behind high walls, some with immense pseudo-Tuscan houses and others with modest, tightly-packed cluster units of relentless symmetry and ugly modernity. You leave the suburbs, the landscape opens up and the greenery is replaced by the flat, harsh brownness of the Highveld countryside, interrupted by billboards announcing plans for even more cluster developments, and high walls around empty fields where these will be built.

You come across a snake park, trout farms, driving ranges, nurseries, kennels, instant lawn farms, paintball fields, wedding venues and Sunday tea havens, the kind of places you might expect in an affluent area that was until recently countryside on the edge of a growing city, and is now seeing rapid urban encroachment. The biggest and most extravagant development is Dainfern, which describes itself as 'Johannesburg's premier residential golf estate offering a secure lifestyle with exclusive recreational facilities'. It sprawls across 800 acres with controlled access, guards on 24-hour patrol and boasts of 'property prices ... in the $2-m range ... an 18-hole golf course, four tennis courts, two squash courts, two swimming pools, volleyball facilities, an oval for soccer, rugby and cricket, and a school.'

A little further along, just before you cross from the outskirts of Joburg into greater Pretoria, the roadside becomes busier and you have to slow down. The sides of the highway are suddenly teeming with people. Along one side you see a solid row of densely interlocked shacks built from metal, cardboard and other scraps, scores of small-scale roadside traders under rough canvas-and-pole shelters, and taxis bouncing around in their disorderly manner on the rough roads around the settlement. An uneven row of portable toilets is lined up by the side of the road, hand-painted numbers on the side of each one, some of them standing at such angles that you wonder at the risks involved in using them. Two buildings loom above the shacks as if to frame the settlement between the imposing symbols of commerce and the state: a new mall at one end and at the other a police station, still under construction.

You have come face to face with the hard reality of South African poverty: a dense forest of shacks, crowds of unemployed people milling on the streets, and attempts by some at small-scale commerce in makeshift shops. Men cluster in groups, throwing dice or playing cards. The place has the dull metal glow of aging zinc housing, the chaos of unpaved roads, the noise of a life lived in packed public areas, the smoke of smouldering braziers and the stench of sewage spilling into the streets. It is stark and bare in the unrelieved dull dryness of a Highveld winter. In summer, at least in rainy summers, it is a lot brighter, greener and softer, with pools of water everywhere.

This is Diepsloot.

From the news media you are likely to know this as a haven for criminals, a place of street justice, and a focal point of the 2008 outbreak of xenophobic violence. You will have heard of regular, and sometimes fierce, bursts of what are loosely called 'service delivery protests' – the poor taking to the streets to ask why their government is not providing the housing and other facilities and services they have promised, often disrupting this very road you are driving on and sometimes stoning passing cars. The most frequent recent mention – at least once a week in the *Daily Sun* – has been when residents resort to rough justice to deal with criminals, making it a centre of mob vigilante action, maybe the global capital.

Diepsloot was in the news in mid-2009 when the Minister of Human Settlements, the flamboyant Tokyo Sexwale, spent a winter's night huddled in one of the shacks to learn about conditions at first hand. The billionaire businessman and charismatic political figure was newly appointed to the cabinet, so it was symbolically important for him to come on one of the coldest nights of the year to one of the harshest parts of this province. It was fine with him, he said, because he had become accustomed to sleeping in the cold when he was a guerrilla. Nevertheless, he stayed four hours of the night and fled back to the suburbs. He brought the media along, of course – there would have been little point in this getting-down-among-the-people display if the cameras had not been there. As a result, the area received more media coverage that week than it had the entire rest of the year. *The Star* called it a 'noble mission'. To residents, it was a milestone – there was the time before Tokyo came, and then there was after. The politician's attention brought hope, the more so that he was senior and a contender for the highest office. With hope comes aspiration and expectation.

The other burst of publicity was the result of the five days of violence aimed at foreigners in early 2008, and the terrible pictures of a mob run amok, which happened in this very same shack area that you see from the road. There was a further attack on Zimbabweans in November 2009. Diepsloot was also the scene of at least two outbursts of political protest, around housing and service delivery issues.

On the website of the agenda-setter of international journalism, the *New York Times*, there is a slideshow titled 'Crime in Diepsloot' –

'Crime is rampant in Diepsloot ... a place where most every door is flimsy and each pathway a peril,' it tells the world. It describes a three-hour attack on a tavern, where robbers played snooker while others carried away crates of beer.

'"Nobody helped," says tavern owner Georges Ndlovu, who was injured in the robbery. "I don't blame them, I would not have helped."'

The slideshow also tells of community courts where citizen volunteers do the work of police. 'They impose fines, they demolish shacks. They sometimes apply beatings.'

Apart from the duo who chase crime stories for the *Daily Sun*, *NY Times* reporter Barry Bearak seems to be the only journalist who spends time in this place, using it as his way of keeping a finger on the pulse of that element of the country which doesn't often feature in the local media.

In late 2008, a BBC programme called *Law and Order* featured Diepsloot as a place of rough justice and rampant crime, a depiction of the country that drew the ire of the South African government because it was seen to be such a partial, one-sided view, only reinforcing traditional African stereotypes.

In the build-up to the 2010 Fifa World Cup, Diepsloot was a convenient location for journalists to tackle the issues of crime and security. On YouTube, a news operation called Euronews had reporter Chris Cummins in Diepsloot, delivering what must be one of the crudest pieces of international journalism I have seen. He speaks to someone identified, mysteriously, as a 'township journalist'. Perched on a pile of tyres on a Diepsloot street, he tells us: 'We could be in another world.' His informant, who shows no credentials and gives no suggestions of how he knows what he says, talks of people taking the law into their own hands, beating and burning alive the criminals, and of dangerous nights, sexual abuse and rampant xenophobia. The piece is filled with horrifying pictures of unstated provenance and murky night-time scenes with Hitchcockian sound effects, all shot from inside a Mercedes-Benz and showing, horror of horrors, lone men walking in the street. Cummins does not talk to one single resident.

The Forced Migration Studies Project in my own university, which investigated the xenophobic violence of 2008, had this to say in a formal academic report: 'The area is also notorious for its history of organised crime and public violence, particularly taxi violence, violent service delivery protest, vigilantism and mob justice.' One sentence containing three references to violence, and crime and vigilantism thrown in for good measure.

This image is felt acutely by those who live in Diepsloot. 'The public perception is that this is a place of violence, toyi-toying from day to day, or taxi violence, or protests against councillors. But from inside, there are dynamics, like any other township that is growing and facing similar problems of migrancy, people who come from all over for education or jobs or to do business,' is how local political leader Chris Vondo puts it. Another resident I speak to says that the criminals dominate the headlines, but apart from that factor, Diepsloot is 'a good place to live'.

Siphogazi Kani, a care-giver, walks around Diepsloot with me for a few hours, visiting households in the direst poverty, and then says, 'So, have you felt threatened?'

Not for a minute, I am happy to concede.

'There is a problem in some areas, like Extension 1, but otherwise things are okay here. We walk around at night till past midnight in my area. But everyone just says Diepsloot is terrible and dangerous.'

Diepsloot, a young hip-hop artist tells me, is '*kwaai*', or cool. He sees it as a place of opportunity, a young and new place where there is space for him to make his name.

Harriet Chauke, a young poet who grew up in Diepsloot and spent two years studying in England, returned to live in the nearby Cosmo City, a place of neat and sterile RDP houses. She comes back here whenever she can. 'I miss the drama of Diepsloot,' she says. 'Sometimes it was unpleasant drama, but I miss it all the same. Diepsloot is alive, it is buzzing.'

This north-Joburg area is also home to a large, ugly, jealous, fussy cannibal with serious parental issues given to occasional, brief streaks of dangerous aggression. This is the Giant Bullfrog, which needs very specific conditions to procreate and finds these in the area of Diepsloot East slated for much-needed new development. It is delaying the building of houses and the pro-vision of services. Officials are having to weigh up the press-ing demand for better living conditions for thousands of people against the safety of this not-quite-endangered amphibian.

The story of Diepsloot is also the story of The Frog.

CHAPTER ONE

'The closer the blacks get, the greener the whites get'

How does an outsider penetrate an area such as Diepsloot? I start, as journalists do these days, on the internet with a virtual tour. Google Maps gives me a bird's-eye view and it is immediately apparent how vast the place is, and how densely populated. When we raced past it along the road we had no idea of what lay beyond the first row of shacks.

In the satellite picture Diepsloot is á dense, dark patch in a sea of surrounding greenery. To the south is a municipal waste water treatment plant and a new cemetery, to the north-west a nature reserve, to the east an open piece of land designated for township development. Main roads run along two sides of it; beyond that on all sides are large-scale developments. It is hemmed in, with only Diepsloot East, on the other side of the R511/William Nicol highway, marked for the people of this overcrowded area.

Through the settlement runs a jagged green stripe, the Jukskei River, or one of its many tributaries. One of these streams – though not the one that runs through the settlement – is called Diepsloot, meaning deep furrow or ditch in Afrikaans and it is this one that gave the original farm its name. It evokes a scar cut into the landscape, and from the satellite picture the Diepsloot settlement is a spreading blemish on the green landscape.

From above, I can also differentiate between parts of Diepsloot. I can see the tightly packed shack areas, but behind them there are some neatly laid-out formal housing areas. And there are places where the two are mixed, with small formal houses surrounded by shacks. There are just a few distinctly middle-class houses, with neat and green gardens.

The roads of Diepsloot all have new South African names, honouring the heroes of the struggle. There is Dr James Moroka Drive, Adelaide Tambo Street, Parks Mankahlana Street, Tsietsi Mashinini Street; even Percy Qoboza and Aggrey Klaaste, two black editors of note, appear to gladden the heart of a newspaperman. These are fallen heroes of the ANC, though some fell victim to drink rather than armed struggle, and some are controversial even in death. It is a sign of the newness of this place, where streets have only been named in the last few years, avoiding those inherited from apartheid structures and the political battles around changing names in other parts of the country.

A comparison with Alexandra, from which many of the Diepsloot people come, tells the story. Alex is an old township nearer to the heart of Joburg, and most of its street names recall colonialists and apartheid rulers: London Street, Vasco da Gama Square, Hofmeyer Street and Roosevelt Street are some of them. As is so often the case, there was a fuss a few years back when just six streets got new names, like Reverend Sam Buti Street, commemorating a local activist. It is hard to change the old, and the new names are a clear sign that Diepsloot is a product of the new South Africa.

That fact is fundamental to Diepsloot. It sprang up in the new South Africa and is not a simple hangover of the old South Africa, where black people coming to Johannesburg were herded into small, overcrowded, poorly serviced areas like Alex, which the government is now struggling to upgrade. In 1994, Diepsloot was a semi-rural farming and leisure area, wide open and sparsely populated; now it houses about 200 000 people. It is a phenomenon of the new era, conceived in the old era, born on the very cusp of change from apartheid to democracy, in that period of transition and uncertainty, a period which began in universal fear and ended in unbridled hope. Like all of this country, it bears the imprint of the past, particularly in its distribution of space and land. It has not been there for long, but in appearance is not unlike the 'black spots' of apartheid, areas of poverty and overcrowding in the middle of cities of wealth and privilege. It is a new settlement but represents also what is not new about this country, what is deeply embedded in the present from a troubled past.

You could start its story any time in the past few hundred years, digging around in that complex history to explain why most of its inhabitants do not have land, jobs or decent facilities, to explain why they are unemployed, why they have moved from elsewhere, why they have come here, why the city is struggling to deal with this settlement and its people, and most notably why such poverty exists alongside Joburg's great wealth. All of this history is written into the place, can be seen at every corner, in every house and on every face, even though the settlement itself is only a few years old. At the same time, it is a place of the new South Africa, a place of hope and possibility, particularly since it does not share the tortured past of similar, older, apartheid settlements. People have come and still come here to claim their place in the new order, to pursue the promises made by a new democratic government, and to seize the opportunities of freedom.

The people of Diepsloot are the cast-offs or refugees of other areas. The immediate story – as I found it in court papers lodged in an obscure corner of the internet – starts in another peri-urban area not far away, called Zevenfontein. Back in 1991 a court ordered the eviction of the small community which had been renting this private land. They had nowhere to go, so they went nowhere, and waged a lengthy political and court battle to find decent conditions and basic services.

There were only 45 families at first, just under 300 people. They were temporarily settled on a piece of adjacent land owned by the Rhema Church, where they became known as the Rhema people. While the court case delayed matters, they were joined in Zevenfontein by others, mostly people coming in from rural areas in search of jobs and opportunity, and their numbers started to swell.

White landowners from the area took steps to try and contain the influx, to preserve the value of their land. 'A tense situation developed', to use the sanitised language of the court documents of the time. The Administrator of the then Transvaal, the old apartheid provincial authority, put together a 'task group' to work out what to do with the Zevenfontein people – or, as the bureaucrats put it, 'to study and report on the means of ensuring orderly long-term urbanisation in the north-westerly quadrant of the PWV region'.

This was a period when the apartheid government had realised it could not stop movement to the city, and could not provide everyone with a house, but could take steps to keep things 'orderly'. It was a time when the bureaucrats, having mastered the building of townships and laying down of 'site and service' schemes, were trying to learn to do it with compassion and care. Experts and stakeholders were duly consulted, and in March 1992 the Transvaal Provincial Administration produced something called the Blue Report, 48 pages long, which set out the problem and potential solutions. This was followed in June 1992 by the 32-page Green Report, which contained specific recommendations as to what should be done with the 'Zevenfontein squatters'. Colourful paperwork was piling up as quickly as the number of squatters in Zevenfontein (which, I was to find, would be the case for the next 15 years).

The Green Report outlined various options: the people could be put in Cosmo City, which was springing up in the same area, or the state could acquire part of the Diepsloot farm and put them there, or indeed split them between this farm and other areas, like Cosmo City or Nietgedacht, also not far away. Moving with haste, just four days later the Provincial Administration expropriated a piece of land, part of the farm Diepsloot 388 JR, 'a certain area of land 92 812 hectares in extent in the District of Pretoria', and cautiously designated land for 'less formal settlement'.

The technocrats sprang into action. The layout plan for the site – which had to be approved before anything further could happen – provided for 1 324 residential sites, each of about 250 square metres, three schools, 16 'community sites', two business sites and 12 parks. It would absorb about half the people now at Zevenfontein, whose numbers had already rocketed to about 8 000. 'What is envisaged is not haphazard squatting, but orderly development within the context of town planning,' they said. People would rent a stand at R58 per month; they would be allowed, initially, to build corrugated iron and cardboard structures, and the main access road would be gravelled. Provision would be made for water, sanitation and electricity, it was promised, somewhat vaguely.

For the government of the time, this was significant: previously they would have recognised only the choice between neat, formal housing and the evisceration of squatter areas; now they were opening a door to something in-between, a pragmatic middle way; an attempt at orderly informal housing with limited services.

The existing landowners of the area were a hot-potch lot, including rabid right-wingers fearing the loss of white political power, small businessmen running light industry on their plots and just wanting to get on with making a living, and New Age vegetable-growers eager to hold on to their tranquillity. They were united by their appreciation of the wide-open spaces, the stark landscape, the semi-rural independence they had established, and the fear of the irreversible disruption that a large influx of people would cause. Many owned modest smallholdings, and the value of their land at the edge of the city was all they had. Some accepted that apartheid had gone and along with it the influx control and land laws which would have prevented black people from moving to the city and occupying such land, while others were determined to fight to preserve what they had.

In the tense and uncertain mood of the early 1990s, the interregnum between Mandela's release from prison and the first democratic election, things threatened to get out of hand. 'A number of militant fringe groups are believed to be mobilising to prevent the community moving to the chosen sites,' a local freesheet, the *Northsider*, reported.

'We will use force to stop the squatters at these sites. If necessary, we will forcibly relocate them somewhere else ourselves,' the chair of the Diepsloot Landowners and Residents' Association, Stuart Aitchinson, told the *Saturday Star*.

'This is going to spark off unholy hell,' said John Stoll, chair of the Anti-Squatters' League.

Louis da Silva of Elandsdrift used the language of a hunter out to cull the squatters: 'I shot one stealing mealies from me once. And if they move here, I will be shooting 10 or 15 every season. I'm not scared.'

Some of the organisations that sprang up were openly racist, some just typically Nimby (Not-in-my-backyard). This was the right-wing in its last burst of pre-democracy muscle-flexing; to them the 'Zevenfontein squatters' represented black hordes encroaching on suburban peace and quiet, the immediate physical manifestation of the invasion of white political enclaves like parliament and the Union Buildings. Some disguised their opposition as a concern for the welfare of the squatters, arguing that people needed proper services if they were moving in; others protested that they posed a threat to the local environment, like the nearby wetland which housed rare frogs and butterflies. 'The closer the blacks get, the greener the whites get,' one unnamed official told a local newspaper.

A Rand Afrikaans University sociologist, Dr Denise du Toit, tried to give academic weight to the argument that you could not put poor blacks and rich whites together: 'Residents of Diepsloot were culturally and socially incompatible with the Zevenfontein squatters, and to place them next to each other would create a potential conflict situation,' she was reported as saying. She was stating the obvious, that putting rich and poor people next to each other was difficult, but her racial slip showed: 'She said the Zevenfontein community was to some extent insensitive to social norms.'

Two white men – including the chair of the Chartwell Residents' Association – were charged with shooting two squatters.

The Chartwell Local Area Committee showed concern – a self-serving concern, of course – when it argued that the squatters should go to Alex, Tembisa and Ivory Park, where they would be integrated into existing communities and services, 'rather than being dumped kilometres from infrastructure and sporting, shopping, educational and recreational facilities'. This quickly brought a response from the Glen Austin Residents' Association, located near Ivory Park, who pointed out that their area was 'fully occupied' and infrastructure was already overextended. People needed facilities, they were all saying, just not our facilities. The white organisations had a voice in the media; the black neighbours they were discussing had not yet found their voice in the new South Africa.

The Transval Provincial Administration, still an apartheid structure but one adapting fast to a new order in which urbanisation was accepted as a reality to be managed, stood firmly by its plan to make this happen in an orderly way. 'No amount of sabre-rattling of the residents in the area will stop [us] from getting on with the job of providing land for orderly urbanisation,' Leon Dekker, deputy-director of Community Development, told the press.

The landowners took the provincial administration to court. In 1992 the Diepsloot Residents and Landowners' Association and an individual landowner named Stuart Aitchinson took on review the decision of the Administrator of the Transvaal to settle people in the area. They argued that the settlement would cause a nuisance and affect their right to enjoy their land. More specifically, they said, the burning of wood and coal would cause air pollution, there would be a marked increase in crime, and the value of their land would diminish.

Before 1990, when white rule appeared impregnable, white landowners might have banked on the courts to protect them from black squatters, but times and the law were changing. Judge J de Villiers granted an interim interdict to stop the settlement, but on hearing the evidence threw the case out and refused leave to appeal. The complainants took it to the Appeal Court, then the highest court of the land, which agreed to hear the case in 1994, but again threw it out, with costs. It found that the law had changed to make it easier to deal with 'squatters', and that the Administrator had acted reasonably and consulted with all parties concerned. The settlement should go ahead.

This had delayed matters for two years, while the Zevenfontein people waited patiently. A well-known journalist, Peter Wellman, spent a night with those waiting to move and described their regular evening meeting to discuss the situation: 'This is no squatter camp where inmates lie around waiting for handouts.' He described an elected committee of 14 coming home from work and setting up a 'community hall' with poles, tarpaulins, a borrowed generator and some lights, bringing chairs from their shacks, to meet from 6 pm to 10 pm to discuss what to do.

The threats of right-wing violence burnt out in the frenzy of the first democratic elections when the landowners came to terms with losing their power to choose their neighbours. The Zevenfontein people would have been buoyed by the hope of the new era and the ANC's 1994 election promise of 'A better life for all'. No doubt they were among the first to stand in queues and cast their first democratic vote in April 1994 in the belief that it would provide their escape from such a precarious position, huddled illegally in temporary shelters on someone else's land without running water or electricity. A vote meant citizenship, the new constitution delivered equal rights, and that surely led to finding a permanent place here on the edge of the city. The ANC's promises of houses, jobs, education, electricity, water, health, security and dignity for all read like this community's shopping list.

The court case was won, but there was still a need to install services before people could be moved if this was going to be properly managed. More patience was required, as always. And the number of people in the settlement continued to go up.

One member of this original group told me that when they heard that other landless people were starting to move into Diepsloot in early 1995, they made a unilateral decision to wait no longer. Emboldened by the new era and a sense that their government had taken power, 'we were not going to let anyone occupy our land. One public holiday, Easter Monday, we packed up our shacks and just went to Diepsloot,' he said.

The following year they were joined by people who had been moved from the flood area of Alexandra, known as the Far East Bank. A second expropriation of land was undertaken in 1996 to accommodate the new arrivals. This meant they were no longer squatters, but had a legal – though vague – status as residents. Combine this with a new government promising houses for all, and it was enough to start a rush. Diepsloot came to be seen as a place of refuge for those flooding into the city from all over, and the promise that those who were there would be eligible for stands or houses was an encouragement. Get in, get a shack, get some space, settle in, and you had a shot at getting on a housing list.

So everyone in Diepsloot is from somewhere, and only some of the very young originate here. Anyone older than 15 has come from a rural area, or a foreign country, or has been evicted from a farm or smallholding in the vicinity, or from Alex, and has been moved to or sought refuge here in the last two decades. A 1996 social survey found that many households had been forced to move to Diepsloot (30 per cent), while others had moved to be closer to their work (27 per cent). The rest came in search of work or housing opportunities. A more recent survey, done by the research agency Case in 2006, found that two-thirds of the residents had arrived within the last five years. An overwhelming 98 per cent said at the time that they did not want to move. They were there to stay – and that was a factor that would shape this community and this area for some time.

If there was to be a sense of community, it had to emerge, for people spoke myriad languages and had a host of different experiences. Again, comparison with Alex is apt, for it is a township with a rich, colourful and proud history. Many great struggle leaders were forged in the bus strike of the 1950s, or the so-called Six Day War, when youths took on the apartheid police in the 1980s. Alex was also home to many newcomers, but it had a core of people who had been rooted there for a long time.

Diepsloot's histories, on the other hand, are dotted around the country. Everyone has a different tale to tell of how they got here: in interviews my most useful first question, 'Where did you come from?' often opened up long and rich personal stories, with no two answers the same.

When people came to Diepsloot is important, as is *where* they were put, and with what services. Those who came from Zevenfontein were put into 1 124 serviced plots in Diepsloot West (no houses, just basic services); Extension One was created when homeless families were moved from Rhema Church land, and they were given neither houses nor services; those moved from Alex were dumped with nothing in what became known as the Reception Area, a shack settlement supposedly for short-term transit, where people would be received before being settled more permanently in other parts of Diepsloot.

These earlier settlers now make it known that they have been there longer than most, and that this imparts prior claim to houses and political status. Certainly, political leaders repeatedly tell me how recently some of their rivals have arrived and how this weakens their claim to hold rank in the community, making them opportunists and chancers. This issue stands alongside the crucial question of when political figures became active in the ANC – the more recently, the more they still have to prove their credentials.

But of course the different services offered created social divisions that still mark the territory. There were those with stronger claims to houses, those who got plots with services, those with plots and no services, and those who just rented space to build a shack and shared services. And they came with political divisions: the Zevenfontein squatters had been divided into three groups: those supporting the ANC, those supporting the Inkatha Freedom Party, and the unaffiliated – and this was reproduced in the location in which they settled. Initially, Diepsloot West had an IFP concentration. Minutes of early Development Forum meetings indicate intense political rivalry and conflict, which even burst into a brief spate of violence in 1995/6.

Create an informal settlement of this sort and what follows is predictable anywhere in the world. People will pay for a shack and a place to put it, and bosses will quickly assert control of the area, selling access and protection to those desperate for it. This form of enterprise is called 'shack farming', a name which carries all the benevolence of pastoral activity, except that it is not sheep or cows being crowded into small spaces and turned around for profit: it is people, and some of the most vulnerable of them.

By 1997, the new city authorities had begun to make plans for housing development and 'de-densification', the polite word for getting rid of shacks. The estimate of 1999 was that there was a housing backlog of 5 000 families, and in the early 2000s the city, working with a private developer named Elcon, developed 4 800 stands. This happened quickly, as it had been identified as a Provincial Premier's special project, with political power and money thrown behind a push to clear all obstacles to getting it done. It did mean, though, that other services – like education and health – lagged behind.

But another 4 522 people were moved from Alexandra in 2001. Alex had been prioritised for urban renewal, and a special presidential project with priority national funding had been set up to fast-track it. To do it, they had to 'de-densify' Alex's informal settlements, and that meant getting rid of the 'undocumented' foreigners and others who could lay no claim to residence there and who were not eligible for the housing subsidies being mobilised to fund building. The problem was exported to Diepsloot, with a R15-million contribution to development from the Alex Renewal Project as a form of compensation.

Others continued to pour in to Diepsloot of their own accord, and the 2001 census counted 49 725 people. By 2005, the official figure was 23 000 families, which would make it more like 90 000 people, but this is undoubtedly an undercounting. Official city estimates now are 150 000 to 200 000 but the figures used by NGOs are at the top limit of that range.

Unemployment is of the highest order, officially measured at 54 per cent of the potential labour force in 2007, with 73 per cent of the people living below the poverty line. Since then, jobs have been lost across the country and the economy moved into recession, so the unemployment and poverty levels are likely to be higher today.

The numbers had overtaken any capacity to build houses there, and people continued to pour in. In 2006, officials said that twice the land area was needed 'only to accommodate the existing backlog in the area and to de-densify the informal settlement'. At that stage, about 80 new people were arriving every day. That is about 30 000 a year. Now, in 2010, about 7 000 additional houses are being planned, probably about a third of the current demand. This is a key to the Diepsloot story: planning has constantly lagged about five years behind reality, and the numbers have shot well beyond what the authorities can deal with. A sewerage system created for a few thousand people now overflows constantly, and 7,5 kilometres of what they call 'daylight sewage' runs largely through the streets. Toilets for 80 houses per hectare were put into the reception area, but by 2010 there were about 270 houses per hectare and so the toilets were overused, abused, and quickly became health hazards. The authorities are trying orderly settlement in a disorderly world.

Closed in by two main roads, with a nature reserve on one side, a sewerage works on another, and upper-income private property developments everywhere else, there is very little space for Diepsloot to expand, particularly with constitutional limitations that make the expropriation of land slow and expensive.

But I am getting ahead of myself. I am still desk-bound and searching on the internet for anything I can find on Diepsloot. A Google search gives me only 104 000 entries, which is about one for every two people. It seems that even in the virtual world,

Diepsloot is marginal. Dainfern, with a fraction of the people, gets 137 000 Google entries.

After a not very informative Wikipedia entry, the next on the Google list is www.diepsloot.com, a site set up and run by residents. 'With this site,' it proclaims, 'our aim is to keep the residents and the world abreast with latest developments in and about Diepsloot and projecting all aspects that make our township to be a vibrant place in South Africa, Africa and the world!' It has pictures of World Cup celebrations in the area, news of a project by the ANC Youth League branches Havana City (Diepsloot) and Rivonia Heroes (Bryanston) to assist schools in the area, calls for entries for Miss Diepsloot 2010 ('Young, slim and intelligent women should enter ... they should have at least matric because winners will get bursaries'), and a piece lamenting the fact that D-Town, as they call it, is not reaping the World Cup bonanza: 'After watching a few documentaries, I discovered SA is mainly Cape Town and Soweto, the other cities don't exist unless it is a scandal or a degrading story, of course ... D-Town obviously does not have much political history or the best site-seeing monument, but we need to be known and our presence felt ...'

I have found a virtual entrance to D-Town.

CHAPTER TWO

The bullfrog with bad attitude

I first hear about The Frog in passing remarks among Diepslooters. Francinah Mbaduli, a community leader, says she has heard that one of the reasons for the delay with construction of new houses is 'some frog or something'. A councillor tells me vaguely that there is an issue with a frog that has to be sorted out – at a consultative meeting a city official had said that the one thing that was not up for discussion was the area that had to be kept for frog breeding. They could discuss the size of houses and plots, the kinds of houses, the space for sports fields, businesses and churches – everything except The Frog. Apparently the meeting moved swiftly on.

It is as if there is some strange presence, like a troll, lurking around the area, to which people will only refer in passing, in a slightly embarrassed way, avoiding it if they can. I struggle to learn more.

An internet search for a combination of 'frog' and 'Diepsloot' draws 13 000 entries (more than 12 per cent of all Diepsloot entries) and the first is Issue 12 of the *Bullfrog Bulletin*, December 2006. This has pictures of volunteers in green World Wildlife Trust shirts attaching cotton bobbins to the backs of huge frogs in Diepsloot. Caroline Yetman, who enjoys the imposing title of Giant Bullfrog Project Executant, is trying a new research technique for tracking the movement of these animals by gluing a bobbin to their backs so that they leave a cotton trail in their wake – cheaper and more efficient than the radio-tracking that researchers usually use, according to the *Bulletin*. The frogs are inspected at regular intervals, 'firstly to check that the frogs were okay and secondly, to check that their bobbins were working properly ... By midnight, both were performing remarkably well, so an end was called to the observation work.' The bobbins stay on only two days, but render some 'incredibly interesting findings' about where the frogs move and burrow.

A nine-page formal letter from Yetman on the letterhead of the University of Pretoria's Centre for Environmental Studies alerts me to the full scope of the problem. When an Environmental Impact Assessment (EIA) was needed for the Diepsloot housing development, she was called in because her doctoral research was based in that area. It had come to her attention, she wrote to the authorities, that the planned Diepsloot East houses 'would threaten the Giant Bullfrog population that uses the three seasonal pans'. She proposed three options to deal with it: protect the bullfrog by creating a buffer zone where there would be no development; relocate them by hand, though they are philopatric (breeding in the same place every year) and the success rate of such removals is very low; or relocate them slowly over 3–5 years, thus postponing the development but raising the chances of success. The first option is most desirable from the frog's point of view, Yetman says, but she is realistic enough to know that it is probably the least likely from the developmental point of view; the latter option is the most realistic and least risky.

The discussion of where The Frog could be moved to brings to light something unexpected: the nearby upper-income Dainfern development had obliterated the bullfrog in its area despite an outcry from environmentalists, but this was in 1992, before legislation made EIAs a compulsory part of the planning process.

Now the people of Dainfern want the frogs back for their golf course, where they can assist in keeping insects in check. The Diepsloot frogs can go there, Yetman suggests. They stand to be the beneficiaries of the most significant class mobility in the area.

Next I find the full EIA, produced by Newtown Landscape Architects in August 2008. They say they are working with Yetman on a Management Plan for The Frog, and introduce a new, benign alternative: make a section of the land an environmental education centre where the frog will be safe and kids can learn about the environment.

Yetman has published a very useful tract on The Frog, 'What you need to know about bullfrogs'. I do not think my need is great, but actually I learn a great deal. *Pyxicephalus adspersus* is the beast's proper name. It is green-brown, about the size of a small football, and makes a soft, deep 'mooing' call not unlike that of a cow. It eats animals ranging in size from flies to small chickens.

Hibernating is what some animals do in winter, while aestivating, I learn, is a summer or year-round activity, or inactivity – when animals live in a dormant state. In the case of The Frog this is as much as 11 months of every year, when it burrows up to half a metre underground, its breathing and heart-rate slow down dramatically, and it seals itself in a keratin cocoon, leaving only its nostrils open. Keratin is the stuff of fingernails or rhino horns.

When the heavy rains come around November, The Frog emerges, sheds this skin and returns to the same place every year to breed prolifically. All breed within 1–2 days of the rains and only in very specific conditions: they need still, shallow water because the female stands in the water but extrudes the eggs in the air, where they have to be fertilised before falling into the water. During this period, the males are 'spectacularly aggressive', attacking one another, sometimes dislodging rival pairs *in flagrante* in fits of jealousy.

Because they need such specific conditions to mate, and Gauteng experiences periodic drought, when they get to do it, they do it furiously, producing thousands of eggs in the hope that a few will survive and make up for those years when the conditions are not quite right.

Once the eggs are laid, a few large males remain behind to defend them, and they do it in a way that would make proud any protective father. They shepherd the tadpoles together to keep them from predators. If the water dries up, the males will dig a large canal up to 10 metres long to connect them with deeper water, and herd them to safety. They pounce on any intruder, such as a human or a horse which comes strolling along. They don't have teeth, but have two bony studs on the sides of their jaws, which they use to deliver a painful bite, particularly effective when a large number of them team up to defend their watery turf. That is, I am told, surprisingly dedicated parenting for such a primitive animal (one still practising external fertilisation). But don't be too impressed. When they get a bit peckish, they eat some of their young. And the young often eat each other: if there is just a slight difference in size, the bigger will eat the smaller, thus contributing to their evolution in size and strength.

Once they have had their fill of their brethren, the surviving froglets hop off quite large distances to find other breeding communities and spread their genes around a bit. The adults spend a month eating themselves silly and then spread out to burrow into the ground and settle in for a long, warm, keratin kip.

So there you have the good life of the Giant Bullfrog: sleeping 11 months of the year, and spending the rest fornicating and eating. And then along comes a developer who wants to build houses. Their breeding ground is the marshy area in the southern corner of where the Diepsloot East development is planned, and their burrowing ground is spread in a large area around that.

Yetman puts me on to Vincent Carruthers, who has come up with a radical new solution to the problem of The Frog and who becomes my primary instructor in these complex matters. I find him in a quaint cottage office in a leafy Joburg suburb. Now retired, he is a passionate lifelong amateur herpetologist, which is what I learn one calls someone who spends time studying big, ugly, troublesome frogs with bad attitude. He is the author of many papers and books on the frogs of South Africa and speaks with the enthusiasm of someone who has devoted many years to an arcane topic and does not often have an interested audience.

Carruthers had rejected the idea of moving The Frog, saying there was no record of success in such ventures, even if done slowly. He suggested instead that that they try to 'herd' it, encouraging it to burrow in a more southerly area, and create a buffer zone for it. He proposed that when The Frog emerged and converged on its breeding water, they put up a fence 800 metres away along the north side, so that it had to burrow closer to the water. This fence would be moved forward 200 metres every year for three years, gradually shifting The Frog southwards. This has never been done before, so it is experimental, and Carruthers is most excited by the prospect. 'I can't wait,' he says. 'I want to see if this provides a solution which can be used elsewhere.'

Through all of this, I presume the fuss is because the beast is endangered. It is, sort of. Globally, it is in the bracket of frogs of 'least concern', because it occurs in a number of southern and East African countries where it is – I can't resist it – safe as houses. In South Africa, it was until recently on a 'near-threatened' list, but now only appears on a Gauteng provincial list of protected animals. The Frog has been progressively displaced by Joburg's northward sprawl over 50 years. In the 1960s they were studied in Blairgowrie, much closer to central Joburg, and that population has clearly been wiped out. Now they cover a much smaller area and it is their misfortune to share a liking for the land of the Diepsloot area with Gauteng urban developers.

I am told The Frog is very tasty, with meaty legs, and that I can buy one for the pot in Diepsloot for about R10. But when I ask someone, he laughs at me: 'I grew up in the Northern Province,' he says, and we used to eat them there. They are quite tasty. But here, we don't eat them. Here, we are civilised.'

Shingai Mpinyuni, of the provincial housing department, tells me that they have incorporated Carruthers' frog-herding regime into their development plans. They will start building in the northern section and work downwards towards the frogs' area in stages, so that there will be 2–3 years for The Frog experiment. The breeding wetland will be left intact and protected.

I learn one more thing which sticks in my mind: frogs are an indicator species, which means they provide us with early warning signs of problems in the environment. They are the aquatic equivalent of canaries in coal mines. Their skins are very absorbent so if, for example, there is a problem with the water they will be the first to die. If you want to know if a place is healthy, I am told, listen for the frogs.

CHAPTER THREE

'No community has experienced development like this'

I meet Phillip Makwela, who runs diepsloot.com, at the Kentucky Fried Chicken outlet in Diepsloot Mall, the large shopping centre which has shot up on the edge of the area. KFC is clearly a regular meeting place: he has commandeered a chair and table, and is casual in Bermuda shorts and a 'Seize Control' T-shirt, a handout of a youth crime prevention programme.

Phillip is chair of one of the two ANC Youth League branches in Diepsloot and is employed as a community liaison officer on a city electrification project. In the evenings, he runs his own business: a marketing and communications company with an interest in websites. Diepsloot.com promotes local business and community and encourages the people of Diepsloot to 'tell their own story'.

Phillip was born up north in Tzaneen and came to Diepsloot with his parents while in primary school. He went to a private school run in the old Diepsloot farmhouse, where he must have stood out because the school owner funded his secondary education at a government school with a good reputation in nearby Randburg. He received a solid enough matric to pursue his ambition to get an electrical or sound engineering qualification from Technikon SA – 'Radio was booming then' – but dropped out after two years because 'it was not me'.

As a community liaison officer, Phillip's task is to facilitate communication between the city structures, a private sector contractor and the community around an electrification project in the area. It is the local authority's practice to hire a local figure to play this role: these projects are often disputed and rancorous in execution. The hiring is done openly, with posts advertised, interviews conducted and CVs scanned, but there are no local media for advertising, so the notices are posted in a few public places and the interviews are done by political comrades. It can't hurt that Philip is a local political leader with ambitions to serve in government structures. Did he get this job because he is politically well connected, or did he gain political weight because he had this job? I was to discover that these things go hand-in-hand.

'When there is a project, the city convenes a meeting to let every stakeholder know about it and discuss the issues: beneficiation, time-frames and so on. Then they come and employ people like me.

'I have the responsibility to do monthly reports for all the stakeholders to know what is happening with the development. If anything is going wrong, I have to explain it to the stakeholders and tell them what has to be done for the development to go ahead.'

He jumps into my car and we drive into Diepsloot proper for him to show me the newly erected street lights and the holes in the ground where others are to be placed as part of his project.

The main road into Diepsloot takes us through what is called 'Government Road' or the 'Government Precinct', where the state authorities have clustered their offices and facilities. The buildings are new and some are still under construction; during my early visits, workers are still putting the finishing touches to the road with neat brick pavements, shiny street lights and a full range of roadside furniture. There is a new police station taking shape, a municipal police depot, an old age centre, a youth centre, a library, a bustling new fire and ambulance station, a taxi rank and a skills development centre.

This stretch of road lasts about 200 metres and then we are in Ingonyama Road, the main thoroughfare, which snakes through the length of Diepsloot. As we leave behind the government buildings and wind through the housing, the road quickly loses its pavements and is left with only dusty dongas on each side, often with big puddles of dirty mud, rocks strewn around and a bustle of people, traders, dogs and chickens.

I am struck by how busy it all is: it is the middle of a weekday morning, but people mill around, well-dressed individuals stride along the street looking as if they are off to work, groups of men sit on crates and talk, traffic moves slowly because of the poor and crowded roads, with unmarked intersections and people strolling across.

The amount of business and trade is overwhelming. Everywhere I look, people are offering goods and services: large grocery or hardware stores rise next to shacks offering hair styles or internet cafes; roadside traders are selling anything you can think of from car and computer parts to clothing, caps and shoes, car wash and car repair; the flash of welding adds to the visual assault of the signs and advertising banners and price lists that are hanging everywhere. Trade is taking place on makeshift tables by the road, from converted shipping containers, and from the windows of shacks. Cellphone businesses are ubiquitous. Many of the larger houses have signs with red crosses saying they are clinics, with a list of what the doctor can offer. There are the signs of building all over: piles of bricks, new and used; bags of plaster, wheelbarrows and cement mixers; half-completed houses.

Taverns and churches are the most common buildings, the

first communal institutions to spring up in a place like this. Life is built around them. 'People in this place are either going to pray or to drink, that's where they meet,' I am told, and they are all over, big and small. There are large and established churches and dozens of small ones that meet in living rooms, garages, tents and open spaces; there are large double-storey thatched-roofed tavern/restaurants and then dark, one-roomed drinking holes in yards. And flapping in the wind in every open space is a large marquee – the tented home of a church, which will be packed out on the weekend. Here is a drive-in tavern, allowing you to pull your car up to a window, order and drive away with a bunch of beers. There are numerous eating places, dark inside and with a few tables out in front, quiet at this time of day. Peer into a dark tavern and young men are playing pool, drinking beer and talking, a television on in a corner. But around and about, there is a buzz of activity. Lots of people, young and old, hanging out. And everywhere the taxis, the ubiquitous 16-seaters swerving all over the road, negotiating the boulders and dongas and hooting incessantly.

Off the main thoroughfare the roads are untarred, full of deep potholes and large, loose rocks. Often a stream of over-flowing sewage runs down the road and people are holding up their trousers and skirts to skip over it. Here, there is a concrete oblong toilet every 20 metres or so along the road, sometimes with a bent and twisted metal door, sometimes locked and freshly painted. As we go deeper into the settlement the road appears impassable and we have to slow down to nothing, swinging from side to side to avoid ditches and rocks. There are few cars, as few cars could navigate such a road. Here the housing is dense with either no vehicle access or small roads running between the shacks, wide enough to take an average car but not wide enough to turn. To get out you have to reverse straight back, avoiding children, chickens and jagged metal jutting out from shacks.

Eventually, the road collapses, it becomes harder to go any further, and then it becomes impossible. People laugh at me trying and wave a finger in a circle advising me to turn around and go back. It looks like this road is many years old and has been washed away after years of heavy use, but Phillip tells me it was re-tarred only eight months previously. The Joburg mayor on a recent visit had been confronted with this evidence of shoddy work by a crooked or incompetent contractor, and had promised to look into it.

Away from the main road, the shops are smaller, but we spot signs for pre-school crèches, a cinema and hairdos in myriad varieties. Many people are sitting on the roadside or in yards, on chairs or boxes, just watching the street life.

This intense activity is very much a part of Diepsloot, and the reason many people express a love for the place, despite its hardships. Harriet Chauke, the young poet, moved from Diepsloot to the more comfortable Cosmo City, where she and her mother now have a house with electricity and water. On Christmas Day, they chose to come to their family here rather than the other way around, because 'it was dead in Cosmo, it didn't feel right'. Her father ran a tavern in Diepsloot before his death a few years ago, and 'it had sometimes been frightening' when they lived in a shack there, she said. But whether it was a fight between a husband and an unfaithful wife, or the discovery of an aborted foetus in a dump, as she put it, Diepsloot was always lively and interesting – and she misses this in the show-piece new housing complex of Cosmo City.

Phillip points out the shiny new poles of his electricity project, beacons in streets of disrepair. 'The only problem we have with our project is with the town planners,' he says. 'They don't know where the pipes are. So sometimes they dig a hole for an electricity pole and hit the water pipe and then there is flooding and the water has to be turned off and people don't have water for a few days. Then I have to make sure everyone knows what is going on.

'It is difficult. I have to fight with people from Joburg Water sometimes.' This is a theme I come across often in the coming months: an inability of different city units to work together, share information and plan as a unit. The result always means a delay, an extra cost, a disruption of services, a hold-up in a project.

Is it a tough job to keep everyone happy? 'Politics will always be politics, but with a development like this no one will be against it. We have to try and handle interests and emotions to say, "Let's manage this". It is a technical development, so no one is against it.'

There is a Contractors' Forum to represent those in the area who can provide services to the project, but this is a sore point: not as many are getting jobs as they would like. Too many have not left the informal sector and do not have the paperwork to get this kind of official task. 'They have to come and make their case to do the work,' Phillip says. 'But the work is technical, so you have to have the skills and the certificates and so on.' He is touching on another difficult issue, perhaps the most sensitive: who gets the work and whether locals have a fair shot at it against large-scale outside contractors. It is a point of serious contention which raises its head in all the interviews I do around these kinds of development projects.

The city does not give him a budget for his work, but if he needs pamphlets or to call a meeting, then he goes to the ward officials who make the resources available.

'We have good councillors,' he says, 'but I will be biased because I am from that organisation that put them there, the ANC.' He knows, inevitably, that I have already heard about severe criticism of the councillors, and even a move to recall one of them, to force him to resign in the manner of President Thabo Mbeki.

I ask him why there have been protests in recent months and he is quick to discount the quotidian explanation of slow government provision of services and development. 'There were no service delivery protests in this area. There was only the Communist Party [SACP] and Sanco [the South African National Civic Organisation] who were not happy with the councillors, because they were not benefiting from the development and some of them were not part of it, and they wanted to get involved in the development.' The SACP and Sanco are governing Alliance partners of the ANC, along with the trade union federation Cosatu, and would not be expected to take to the streets to protest against a government they are part of. Sanco is a loosely-structured civic organisation deeply embedded in Alexandra, where it played a central organisational role in the resistance of the 1980s, and came across to Diepsloot with those who moved from the older township. The SACP is made up of more hard-core cadres, with a mission to move the ANC to the left and focus attention on the poor and jobless. It is immediately apparent in Diepsloot that the relationships between these organisations and the leaders who run them are at the centre of local politics.

Following the protests, the ANC has moved to develop closer links with its political critics within the alliance. 'We now have engaged with them, and we make sure the councillors don't run alone. The city people came and spoke to everyone, so things are okay for now, but tension might rise because we are heading for local government elections, and everyone is trying to position themselves to be councillors,' Phillip says.

There are other political parties in this area, but their presence is small and the action is all between and among the ruling Alliance partners. 'In this area, there is the Inkatha Freedom Party, and there is the slowly-dying Cope [the ANC breakaway], and there is the [liberal] Democratic Alliance. But we have no relations [with them]. We can't be fighting, but there are no relations. With the DA, it is very hard, because if you are part of them then you are recognised straight away as a sell-out. And the IFP, it is slowly dying.'

In a few brief paragraphs, he has laid out Diepsloot's basic political geography. The DA might be the official parliamentary, provincial and city opposition, but it is stigmatised – to be seen to be with it is to be seen to be a traitor to the struggle. The ANC has established hegemony, but is locked in a complex and fraught relationship with its Alliance partners. It is the battle within the ruling grouping which defines local politics, fought over access to the development projects and the work they offer to this community.

The politics is inward-looking: at no stage in Diepsloot does anyone express concern to me that they are surrounded by such ostentatious wealth, that they are still perched on the city's so-cial and economic periphery, that their relationship with their neighbours is an issue. The political battles are all between those within the community who have access to at least some resources and those on the periphery of the periphery, who are excluded from the fruits of development.

Phillip juggles three caps – as a local political figure, a com-munity liaison officer and an aspirant businessman – and he does so with ease. He is self-conscious about leadership, citing the burdens and responsibilities it carries, and the opportunities it presents to him, in a language I hear frequently in coming weeks. He talks as 'one of the leaders', and this involves certain attitudes, behaviours and tasks. Ask him about rumours of ris-ing xenophobia, and he will tell you that there is a need to be vigilant and to 'engage' the community to try and get them to see that dealing with illegal foreigners must be left 'to those tasked with this', namely the police. And leaders must get peo-ple to see that we need the skills of the immigrants who are legal, 'so they can also teach us skills'. Community problems have to be 'managed' and communication is at the centre of it. It takes a while to get him to express personal, non-official views.

He is soft-spoken and thoughtful about what he says. I discover Phillip as a man of principle, who is not afraid to speak out when he thinks something is wrong, but who always does so from the perspective of the party. Part of the reason for the caution he shows is that he sees his future on a distinctly political path through the ANC: 'With the election next year, some of us will be absorbed into government at a local level. Now I see myself as a businessman, wanting to grow my business, employ people and improve lives. On the political side, we need to grow as well, making sure we are part of the service delivery chain.'

The battle for position and all it entails becomes a major theme in all political discussions in the coming weeks, showing me how deep these conflicts run and how bitterly they play out within and among an intertwined set of political and community organisations. Probing the politics of Diepsloot is like trying to find one's way through a hall with lots of doorways: I find many open doors, each one offering a different path into Diepsloot, but each one revealing more doors behind them, and more behind those. And all these rooms are inter-leading, maze-like.

I quickly learn that the impression I got from the periphery of Diepsloot of wall-to-wall shacks, absence of services and unalloyed poverty was simplistic. There are four types of housing in Diepsloot, and to see the difference is to start to understand the structure and stratification of the township.

There is the informal housing, dense and congested shacks which hold the majority of people (70 per cent in the 2001 census), with shared water and sewerage facilities and no electricity. The toughest of these is called the Reception Area, because it is where all newcomers were put before getting a house or a piece of land in the surrounding extensions. It was temporary, and 15 years later people are still stubbornly sticking with that description, still trusting in the promise of proper housing and services. Spreading outwards from this core, there are places where people were given pieces of land with some basic facilities, and they provided their own housing, usually a mix of informal and formal, the product of the original government scheme to allow for 'less-formal' but 'orderly' settlement.

There is the new government's hand-out RDP housing, named for its initial Reconstruction and Development Plan, now long abandoned though the pattern of housing remains. These are small matchbox-style houses with a floor space of about 38 square metres in the middle of regular square stands, of which about 5 000 were built in 2001, with full services. These have been delivered as a government turnkey project and come – after long bureaucratic processes – with title deeds.

And finally there are 'bond' houses, those built by independent developers for better-off residents who can finance them through bank bonds and often with the support of an employer, and which range in size and comfort. None are huge, but these houses stand out, neat and tidy and often with well-tended gardens and tiled roofs – a requirement, I later learn, to get a bank bond.

It takes a practised eye to see the difference between the informal and much of the RDP housing. Most of the new houses have shacks packed into their small yards, increasing the density again and hiding the formal government-issue house in the middle. I have to look for the signs of services, such as electricity and toilets. But they are there. The 2001 count put only 24 per cent of the residents in brick structures, 43 per cent in shack areas, and 27 per cent in backyard rental shacks.

Courtesy of a friendly builder, I climb on the roof of a two-storeyed house being constructed on a hill and look down on an unbroken agglomeration of brick and cement and zinc structures, often with a tangle of home-made electrical wiring hanging between them like badly cooked pasta.

It takes me a while to understand what this sight is telling me: people have been given houses and space, but most can't afford them without renting out a part, adding rooms, stringing up illegal electricity supplies, making space for their families or for tenants, perpetuating many of the conditions the government housing scheme was meant to eradicate. It is a hive of half-finished, apparently lackadaisical building operations, with many people adding on to their houses, often doing it themselves. Piles of old, used bricks are a common sight as people harvest material from building sites around Joburg. Dangerous electricity connections are epidemic.

The occasional house stands out: face-brick, perhaps double-storeyed, with a fancy, hand-painted wall, or an elaborate metal gate, or a neat, well-tended garden. Here is one with a smooth lawn and neat rows of roses and hydrangeas. There is one that rises to three floors, with a kind of turret at the top, looming above the small RDP houses and shacks. But they are the exceptions.

It is impossible to hold on for long to the naive idea that Diepsloot is a simple, homogeneous community. Some 35 per cent of houses told the census-takers in 2001 that they had no household income at all, while at the other extreme some 70 houses (0.3 per cent of the population) declared an annual income of R153 000 or higher. I discover pretty quickly that this place is made up of many communities with some things in common – like a need to fight crime – but many different and divergent interests, defined by when people arrived, whether they have jobs, whether they have acquired title to their property, whether they get government grants, whether they have access to the resources of power and development, what their nationality is, and where they live within Diepsloot.

People are quick to say which part of the settlement they live in, expressed as an extension number. It is significant, because – like any suburb – it reveals a bit about the person, but it is complicated to understand because there are names on the maps and there are names that people use, and these are not necessarily the same. The Reception Area is where people were originally settled temporarily, but remain. It is the most dense area, with the worst services. Diepsloot West is where the first houses were built, the first push to turn informal into formal settlement, with 1 124 houses – and now with some 4 000 backyard shacks. The Elcon development area, with some 6 000 houses, covers Extensions 1, 2, 3, 5, 6, 7 and 9 (though many people use Extension 1 and Reception Area interchangeably). Tanganani can refer to one of the original areas, where there is now bond housing, or the planned new housing area of Diepsloot East. There is the Mayibuye Housing project, where 700 houses were built on serviced land. And now there is a new area, where people have been made to move to accommodate the rebuilding of the sewerage system in the township, perched on a hill on the edge, called Extension 12 or Adelaide Tambo. It is uncertain how the genteel wife of the former ANC leader, who spent much of her life leading the struggle in exile from Muswell Hill, would feel about being memorialised by this temporary, informal, marginal, barely serviced centre of poverty and symbol of neglect. But for the residents, the move there was not without its benefits: they were given demarcated space, allowing them to fence off their little piece of land and improve their stands, and a toilet for each shack. They still don't have electricity and they share water taps, lined up over a trough at one end of the street, but they have taken a half-step up from Extension 1.

In Extension 3, there are some neat gardens, green front verges and even one house decorated with an extravagant display of topiary. In one place, I find a traffic circle with a fountain and well-kept lawns and flowers. It was built and is maintained by a man living in one of the surrounding houses, I learn later, and he is out every day watering and tending it. This contrasts strongly with the Reception Area, where the density is overwhelming, the sewage smell takes some getting used to and the mood is relentlessly harsh and busy. In August 2008, fire broke out, 23 shacks burnt down and 100 people were left homeless. It is easy to see how fire can rage uncontrollably though these parts.

Winding through the settlement is a branch of the complex of streams and rivers known as the Jukskei River, which springs up under Ellis Park stadium in central Joburg and runs north-west through every element of the city – rich suburbs where houses fortunate enough to look over it garner premium prices, and crowded informal settlements where the rains bring flash floods and regular, predictable disaster to those huddled on its banks. The river draws the attention of the independent churches of the poorer areas, for some of whom it has sacred baptismal qualities, as well as the suburban greenies, who from time to time rally volunteers to clean it up and campaign for it to be re-habilitated. By the time the river trickles into Diepsloot, it is foul and rank brown-grey water, filled with plastic rubbish, smelling of sewage and laden with health hazards. Nothing could live in it, or at least nothing you would want to live beside. *E. coli* levels reach super-toxic heights as sewage flows into it. From the satellite picture, it seems to provide a green lung running through the area, trees and bush on either side, but close up it is dirty and dangerous, with children balancing precariously on loose rocks and rotten planks thrown down to enable them to cross it.

It is as if all the detritus of industrial Joburg has been dis-charged into the river as it snakes through Diepsloot. In the rainy season, it turns hostile: in 2006, 400 families had to be relocated out of the floodplain when 34 shacks washed away, and one woman was drowned. But it is evident that new people came and occupied the flood plain, desperate for land. Houses run right up to the river, precariously balanced on eroding banks, and when the summer rains come, there is no doubt they will be washed away. A big, bold sign saying 'Beware flash floods!' a few metres from the river stands above shacks built right on its edge.

There is one healthy green lung in Diepsloot: a television park, fixed up for the 2010 World Cup. It is fenced, lawned, a row of carefully tended rose bushes down one side, with neat rows of benches, a brightly painted playground with swings and roundabouts, and a giant outdoor television screen resplendent in the banana yellow of the cellphone company that sponsored it. During the day it broadcasts cartoons and kids' programmes, dim in the sunlight, but it is sport that brings the crowds. For the World Cup, it was not a great success, I am told, as it was extremely cold and the screen repeatedly seized up. The park remains, however, as one of the few World Cup legacies for this area and on weekends and public holidays it is alive with families picnicking and children racing around the playground.

Notably absent in this area is public transport other than the occasional bus and private taxis. There is no railway for people to get to workplaces, and only a skeleton bus system. A student who has to be at Wits University at 9 am joins the queue for taxis at 6 am to get to the campus just on time. There are plans to bring the new city rapid transport system, Rea Vaya, here. This holds out the promise of transforming people's ability to get to work, therefore to find jobs and so afford the housing and services being provided. But it also holds out the prospect of taxi wars, as the taxi drivers are king of these roads. There already has been a mini-war over control of routes, back in about 1997. Still the taxi drivers behave with the arrogance and disregard which comes with controlling the roads and knowing people are dependent on them. One volunteer worker who comes here often in a taxi-like vehicle tells me how one day the taxi-drivers, mistaking her for unauthorised competition, all suddenly boxed her vehicle in, climbed out of their vehicles carrying weapons and threatened her, until one driver recognised her, and got the others to back off.

Phillip is the exemplar of a new stratum of semi-professional politician I encounter in Diepsloot. He is the first I come across, but there are a number of others – such as the two ANC branch chairs, Rogers Makhubele and Chris Vondo – who fit a similar description.

They are the progeny of Mandela, in that they were young when he was released and are rising now, in their twenties and early-to-mid thirties, into and through local leadership positions and headed for provincial and national political leadership, or to be deployed into public service, probably a combination of both. They do not have the baggage of the older activists, for whom the pains and gains of the struggle are still fresh, yet they are intensely loyal cadres, whose lives and views and relationships have been shaped by Mandela's ANC.

They are usually employed in some way by state structures, or 'deployed' there, as they would put it, often at a provincial or local level. The ANC has a policy that to effect transformation and break the hegemony of white males, it needs to place loyal comrades in positions of influence in all parts of South African society, public and private. To do so, it has a dedicated 'Deployment Committee' in its Luthuli House head office.

Most of the Diepsloot political leadership earn their livelihood through some form of public service deployment, though many speak of their businesses on the side. These businesses often seem to be an aspiration rather than a reality, but what sets these individuals apart from most in Diepsloot is that they have jobs, almost always in public service. Their ANC involvement is a path into public service, and in turn it often gives them resources and patronage they can use to chart their way. They tend to have more education than most in their area, but not a lot of tertiary qualifications. Some have come through the ANC Political School and followed a set path into and through the party: they have shown leadership in an educational, sport or church structure, become active in the Youth League, risen to a position of local standing, gone through ANC 'training', and then been recommended on to a city or provincial ANC position – from where they have the potential to go to the national level. It is structured and measured: nobody goes forward without climbing through the ranks, and the steps on the way up are clearly set out.

The ANC is not just a political party, it is the party of liberation. At almost a century old it is proud of being the oldest political party in Africa, but is more like a church, a broad and embracing family which offers support, succour, mentorship and opportunity. At each stage, would-be office-bearers have to show commitment, loyalty and an understanding of the responsibilities of leadership. There is a deep ANC culture, and it shapes how they behave, how they compete for position and how they bear the burden of leadership. In exile, the ANC was not just a meeting point, a gathering of like-minded rebels, but it fed and housed and nurtured its members, who now have a loyalty of great intensity. These youngsters don't have that, but they do feel the weight of that history and the nobility of the struggle culture.

Nobody starts out on an ANC path without first learning the rules, the history, the 'culture'. These protocols of political civility were born of the mission-school gentlemen who started the ANC and nurtured it through exile, but they now have to contain the morass of political infighting that comes with winning and holding power, with competing for access, position and resources, with managing patronage. The ANC's public debates these days reflect the battle between this history and the brash new culture of young upstarts who believe they are emulating the rebellion of Mandela's Youth League of the 1950s that radicalised the organisation in that period.

On the ground in Diepsloot the leadership – including the youth leadership – presents itself as responsible, thoughtful, cautious and concerned. There is not a lot of bling. There is no cheap populism, at least among these office-bearers. Rather, there is a strong sense of the responsibilities and burdens of leadership, the need to manage expectations and demands, and to convey a realism about service delivery.

These young leaders are, however, determined to drive forward the push for transformation and service delivery to the poor which has so often seemed to stall in the new South Africa. Phillip is a supporter of outspoken ANC Youth League leader Julius Malema as someone who speaks his mind and tackles issues he feels the ANC leadership tiptoes around, and on which it panders to foreign or wealthy interests at the expense of his constituency. But he is not comfortable with Malema's cruder outbursts and what he views as his less educated pronouncements. He criticises Malema for calling opposition leader Helen Zille a 'cockroach'. He says tactfully that education is an important part of leadership, and doesn't need to make the point that Malema is a high school drop-out. But he will support Malema's re-election to a second term as Youth League President largely because it is part of a wider plan to put a stronger leadership in place in the ANC.

The Youth League members of Diepsloot are conscious of themselves as the 'kingmakers of the ANC', those who put current President Jacob Zuma into power and can make or break him. They have already decided that Zuma will not get a second term, as he has failed to keep his more radical promises, and to back deputy president Kgalema Motlanthe as the next national leader, contrasting his moral stature and willingness to take a stand on tough issues with Zuma's prevarication on all fronts. Phillip criticises Zuma for playing to an international audience, citing the fact that he rejected the idea of nationalisation of the mines while in England even though it was under discussion in the ANC back at home, and attacked Malema as a precursor to travelling to the United States, where he knew he would face questions about the youth leader.

43

At public meetings, 'Long live Malema' almost always comes before 'Long live Zuma' in the ritual call-and-response chanting.

The Diepsloot Youth League leaders also see themselves as 'kingmakers' in the local context: those who have the energy, drive and commitment to run the ANC structures in Diepsloot and influence what happens. They hold this position through dint of hard work: speaking of all-night meetings and strategy sessions before public meetings or political interventions. They see themselves as leaders with their base built at branch level, earning their stripes in on-the-ground politics among their people. They talk of 'service' and more than once I was told that local political leadership was not a career but a 'calling', like the priesthood. The future of the ANC is probably in the hands of these loyal cadres, waiting to be deployed into all sorts of positions to displace those they consider old-guard and insufficiently part of the national democratic revolution.

'We have been on the ground, we know the issues and problems,' Phillip says. Government is run by professionals, and that is good, nothing wrong with that when they do their jobs, but they are not under pressure to deliver. 'We know the needs of the people. We feel the pressure because we are here on the ground.'

They have learnt the frustrations of government and, naturally, they push the idea that to cement the national democratic revolution (NDR), the ANC has to get its cadres – people like themselves – into key positions in state structures to implement policies and replace an old guard of 'professionals' who are just doing a job without the necessary passion.

'The councillors don't have the power; they depend on officials who are professionals,' Phillip says. 'When I am a politician I say what has to be done, but the officials are not under pressure to do it until people start to riot. We voted for Zuma, but he does not control some of these things we are talking about, because there are people there who are not deployed, they don't understand what is needed, sometimes they don't even want these things, they are just professionals doing a job.'

He is expressing the discovery that government is slow and difficult to change; that patience is required; that it is one thing to win and hold power, another to use it effectively. The reference to professionals in government is careful, polite wording. He is talking about white bureaucrats inherited from the past, many of them experienced and competent, but whose commitment to the ANC agenda is uncertain.

These party cadres are the interface between government and those on the ground who put the government there and who have been promised the freedom dividend. It is these local leaders who have to face protestors and unravel the complex politics of the branch. It is they who have to 'manage' their complex constituencies.

They do it well. The ANC branch for Ward 95, the Havana City Branch, was the 2009 ANC branch of the year. It is the proud holder of the Sol Plaatje Award for Best Performing ANC Branch, announced at the ANC annual 8 January birthday bash. The award is not judged on numbers, fortunately, for it is not a big branch, but on unspecified issues of performance.

Diepsloot is bisected into two political constituencies, Wards 95 and 96 (the latter changed to Ward 113 in the 2010 demarcation) and this means two councillors, two branches, as well as two arms of the Alliance partners with a presence here, the SA Communist Party and Sanco. Relations between and among all these groupings – even ANC branches and councillors – are tense. A complaint I heard often was that one ANC councillor was venturing into affairs in the neighbouring ward. Likewise, I often heard Sanco leaders in one ward distance themselves from those in the other ward. Much of this was expressed in terms of personal differences and questions of individual behaviour, rather than ideological divides.

Rogers Makhubele is a go-to man in Diepsloot. I meet him at the city social services office, where he has a room opened up for us to sit in. Now 36 years old, he grew up in Giyani, Limpopo, where he matriculated and showed his potential in two terms in student council leadership. In search of greener pastures, like so many people from smaller towns, he joined his brother in Alexandra, and followed him to Diepsloot around 1998. Ignoring his brother's imprecations, instead of going out to seek work he hung out with the local politicians and structures, knowing somehow that his place was among them. He worked his way through ANC Youth League local leadership into the ANC proper, and is now in his third term as branch chair. He is proud of his qualification from the ANC Political School, particularly the 100 per cent he achieved for the module on governance.

Rogers' loyalty was sorely tested during the previous round of council elections in 2005. He was put forward as the ward candidate, but then 'I was out for political reasons,' he says. Asked to explain, he will only add, 'You know, in these local politics, people complain and object and sometimes you have to stand aside.' He is being cautious, tactful and loyal.

One of his colleagues later tells me the full story and it is a powerful illustration of how fraught are the contestations for these posts: his was number two on the list of three names put forward by the branch as candidates for the approval of the ANC at provincial and national level. This is a contentious mechanism put in place because of concern about the quality of some candidates in the early years of democracy. Also, it allows head office to ensure that the election lists achieve a racial and gender balance. It is contentious because it puts control of the most basic function of the branch – the nomination of candidates for office – into the hands of party officials. If not used sagely, it disempowers branches; either way, it complicates selection, requiring candidates simultaneously to curry favour downwards, among their branch members, and upwards, among party officials.

In the selection process that blocked Rogers, the first candidate was popular, but had only been a member of the ANC for a year and failed in her interview at ANC headquarters to name the secretary-general. It was a cardinal political blunder in a party so steeped in history as this one and on the lookout for chancers, newcomers and opportunists. She was rejected and Rogers was next in line. On the day all the city candidates were called together for a photograph, a letter arrived at the ANC office alleging that he was a dagga-smoker and dice-player. The ANC was trying hard to clean up the ranks of its local candidates, and they wouldn't take the risk of having a street skollie in the council. He was pushed aside for a person dismissively described as 'a taxi-driver', Madlozi Ndlazi. Rogers is coy on the subject, but I learn from others that he toyed with membership of other parties, particularly Cope, but has since cleared his name and stayed on as ANC chair, hoping for another shot at the title.

The winning candidate, Ndlazi, when I meet him later, recalls from memory the branch voting, perhaps indicating how important he finds it to legitimise his election. He puts himself at second place, and therefore the rightful heir to the post rather than the third in line. There were five candidates, he says: Susan got 35 votes, he got 28, Rogers got 15, Sarafina got 12 and someone called Mangana got just 1. The most striking thing about this, though, is the low number of votes. All branch members can vote, so it was surprising how few were active enough to participate and how it was decided by just a handful of people. He also has a different version of what knocked out the winner: 'Susan couldn't be councillor of the ANC because she had a bad record of being arrested, leading marches and riots in Diepsloot,' he says.

Chris Vondo, the other ANC ward chair and the first person

to tell me Rogers' election story, uses it to show me the true loyalty of a comrade. 'It was hard for him but he is still with us, still working,' he says. In 2011, he is being rewarded by being lined up to be the city councillor.

Rogers is reluctant to express his ambition, in line with the ANC ethos that candidates do not thrust themselves forward but wait to be nominated at the right time and in the right way. ANC candidacy is a question of finding a delicate way to make oneself available without ever saying it publicly. 'I won't stand again [as ANC chair]. You need to grow as an individual. You need to use what you have learnt at another level. I will continue to serve the organisation and the people. But we don't put ourselves forward, we depend on the mandate of the organisation.

'It also isn't about leading always from the front. Remember, we had the likes of Walter Sisulu who led from the back but was an important thinker and strategist.'

Rogers talks a great deal about the need for 'process', going through the 'correct procedures', doing things in the 'right way', the need for 'patience' and the important role of leaders to get people to understand these things. It is a common organisational and managerial language I hear from local ANC leaders, one that betrays their awkward placement between those expecting the rewards of freedom and those responsible for their delivery.

'People are in a hurry [for houses], but processes must be respected,' he says. How long will the new housing development planned for Diepsloot East take? I ask. 'We cannot put a timeframe on it. It is a triple-P (a public–private partnership) and we need to look at it closely. We have to go through the right procedures.'

What are the central issues to be addressed to speed up delivery? 'We have a problem of land availability. If we can have land, it will make a difference, but we need to educate our people. When you have land, then what?

'People need to understand the processes, the government processes. We have land in Diepsloot East, but we need to give the provincial government and the city [a chance] to follow and conclude the processes that need to be followed.

'We are not looking to build shacks, or just RDP houses, we also need to accommodate bond houses, so you can create revenue through water and lights and rates, so that this area can sustain itself ... We expect this to be the kind of development where there will be life, you need schools, sports fields, all you need for a viable community.'

Rogers has a construction company, but it has not been active for a couple of years. 'There are many concerns about conflict of interest, so as a leader you cannot look like you are channelling work for yourself. When we talk of the problem of corruption, we have to lead by example.

'But,' he adds wistfully, 'we also have a right as citizens to participation in these business opportunities ...'

In the meantime, like Phillip, he has been employed by the local authority as a community liaison officer. He speaks passionately against 'individualism': his sharpest criticism of some of his colleagues and rivals is that they are pursuing personal agendas and putting themselves above the organisation and its broader interests. Or to put it another, grander way, they are putting themselves above the sacred National Democratic Revolution, as represented by the ANC.

'Diepsloot is at work,' he says. 'It is a young place but there is no community that has experienced development like this. We have all the structures a community can acquire: a library, a police station is being built, a Joburg Municipal Police Precinct, emergency services, the Early Childhood Development building, a skills development centre, schools, halls, two clinics, the social services centre where the government departments come once a week so people can access their services, an old age centre ... There is lots happening here. We have just installed 250 toilets in Extension 1 with running water, Diepsloot East is under way where they will build 9 000 houses.

'There has never been a stoppage in development here. It has been going on all the time.'

Currently, he adds, the Joburg Development Agency is upgrading the main road into the township and redoing the problem part (where it has washed away). They are building two pedestrian bridges to cross over the streams.

'The community came up with this [the bridges] and said it was a priority. It is not really safe, especially for kids going to school, when there is rain or at night. I am happy that the Joburg Development Agency is responding to this,' he says.

Rogers will acknowledge some delays caused, interestingly, by the country's hosting of the 2010 Fifa World Cup: 'The road should have been done already – they are only doing phase one now – but because of the budget and because of the World Cup it has been delayed. It was meant to be done this year, but the government made the call that the departments had to give focus to 2010 developments, so the budget had to be diverted. But now it will continue.'

He has little time for those who complain about poor service delivery. 'Whoever is raising these issues, these are people pushing their personal agendas. On services, the city has been working as hard as it can.

'We are becoming a real community; our people have come together over these things. There are just a few elements who are trying to disrupt this government of the people.'

Aren't people impatient? 'Only those who are opportunists, who have other reasons, political or whatever, who can take advantage. Since 1995, people have been patient, so I see no reason why people won't continue to be patient.'

I was to hear these two things frequently in my first few days in Diepsloot: ANC leaders saying there was no place which had seen faster development than this one, and that those who complained about it had 'their own agendas'.

Who are these disruptive people? In a bid to push him on this, and get past vague references to those who oppose, I ask about relations with the ANC's Alliance partners. 'It depends. Alliance leaders push their own agendas in some places.

'There is not a good relationship at local level here, because of individuals pushing their own agenda, who see an opportunity to pursue their own interests in the ANC. It depends on the individual. We have ethics in the organisation, we have policies and rules. There is no space for any individual who see themselves as bigger than the organisation.

'Sometimes there is intolerance, hatred, lack of understanding. Others want to take short-cuts and then some of us say, no, that is not what we stand for. To others, it does not go down well.

'But so far we have been able to manage that. In politics, it is not about agreeing on everything. We are autonomous structures. The ANC will always lead but there is space for the alliance members to raise issues of concern. But it should be raised internally.'

A bit more of a push and he starts to talk more frankly. Sanco leaders, he says, held a public meeting where they called for foreigners to leave this place, raising the spectre of further xenophobic violence. Sanco leaders deny this, but not that they lay behind protests. 'There are people who do not want to follow proper processes,' Rogers says. 'They only want mass action and toyi-toying without even getting permits for these marches. They are trying to make this community ungovernable. So the relationship is sour [with Alliance partners, meaning Sanco and the Communist Party, as there is no Cosatu presence].

'It is a pity they use our organisation's colours. Some of them are just using their membership to pursue their personal objectives.' Are the councillors part of the problem?

Only one of them, in his view. 'We have a councillor who is

not up to scratch, who is pushing a lot of his family. The organisation will look at that. He is dividing the community.'

He will only say that the problem is not the councillor of Ward 95, with whom they have good relations. By implication, it can only be Ward 96's Isaac Maella.

I was beginning to get a sense of how fraught are the tensions and rivalries that characterise these positions. As I dig into these issues, the language becomes harder and the tone increasingly bitter.

People tell me that someone who will talk candidly about Diepsloot politics is Chris Vondo, chair of Havana City branch of ANC, Ward 96, the branch of the year.

'Consolidate the gains of the national democratic revolution,' is his telephone message, an echo of the ANC's 2009 slogan. Chris works as coordinator of government business in the Office of the Premier and is 'very active' in the Gauteng provincial executive of the ANC Youth League. He lives in a small but well-furnished bond house with a neatly kept yard, unusual in that it is not occupied by sub-tenants.

Before we meet, he has to run to open a workshop about the launch of the Diepsloot Front Against Xenophobia, planned for Mandela Day, two days away. At the meeting, it is clear that he is the leading figure, and he immediately assumes the role of informal chair. Then he excuses himself to talk to me and asks the council officials to make an office available for us. He is loquacious, full of thoughts and ideas and bubbling with intellectual energy and passion for the national democratic revolution, jumping from topic to topic.

'Diepsloot is one of those communities growing on a daily basis because it is new. Therefore it has become very difficult to manage, politically and developmentally,' he says.

Chris arrived here in 1997 from the Eastern Cape, and has been involved since then in the issues of Diepsloot. When the first RDP houses were built in the early 2000s, he was a part of the Community Development Forum (CDF). 'I was Youth Co-ordinator in CDF that was instrumental in this project when we built 4 500 RDP houses and 1 000 stands. Implementation was very difficult, there were a lot of dynamics in the process where the political and social structures clashed on these things … Where there are shacks people are not patient, and they can be mobilised.'

It was the grouping 'that called themselves Sanco', as he puts it, who were behind the protests. Their leaders were unemployed, and they therefore made their living by exploiting the shack situation, he argues.

'In 2001, there was a protest from that group when people were coming from Alex. Because of the lack of space there, they came here. Government committed to build infrastructure in the Reception Area, like toilets and water from the funds of the Alex Renewal Programme. But these same people, maybe because their leaders are unemployed, want to exploit the situation, want to put people in shacks in a way that is very congested. The Pikitup [city garbage removal] trucks can't get in. There are shacks all over and when they tried to move shacks to open the roads, the people were mobilised to toyi-toyi.

'They say they want development, but when it comes they oppose it.'

The Sanco chair, a man known only as Letsoalo, comes up often at the heart of these issues. Letsoalo is the powerful leader of those in shacks, particularly in the Reception Area. He was granted a formal house in the first batch built, I am told, but refused it, saying people did not want these 'matchbox houses'. The real reason, his critics suggest, was that he did not want to leave his political and financial base in the shacks.

'He has been instigating these things, but we are trying to engage with him,' Chris says.

The core of the problem, according to Chris, is control over the densely packed shack area. 'One of the main challenges – if the government can see to it, we will not have these problems – is the dismantling of the Reception Area.' I am startled by the harshness of this evocation of apartheid language, but later he softens it: 'If the Reception Area can be de-densified, as planned originally, the problem will be solved.'

He paints a picture of mob rule in these areas: 'In the Reception Area, there is mob justice. People are sjambokked, they take rent when they are not supposed to, people are asked to pay for protection, especially the Pakistani shop owners. They are terrifying them. Block F is notorious, it is where the leaders are concentrated,' he says.

For him, the lack of education and employment in the leadership is a core problem. It means that they want to use their positions for personal gain, and their control over these areas is their source of livelihood.

And then he launches into an attack on one of his own ANC councillors, the same one that Rogers had laid into. '[Councillor Isaac] Maella is part of the problem. He is deputy secretary of my branch. He apologises at meetings, does not provide reports, he is seen to be preoccupied with the local government elections, he goes to the other ward where people once toyi-toyied against him.

'They wanted to recall the councillors, they were sending letters to the president of the ANC on Youth League, Sanco and Communist Party letterheads. We had to intervene, there were barricades in the street, there was looting. We went onto the street, said we would fight fire with fire. They said I was going to be killed. They were not raising these issues in the proper way. They copied the Sakhile people [an Mpumalanga township that saw high-profile and quite violent service delivery protests, where the national leadership came in and sacked the councillors]. Then they copied Alex on the xenophobia stuff. They called a meeting, they were stopping taxis to ask if there were foreigners on them. They saw what happened in Alex and thought national leadership would come here, they called for the recall of the mayor, saying there was a problem of service delivery.

'We said there is no problem of service delivery here, there is massive development in the area: schools, mall, taxi ranks, lots of investment by government. There is no place in Gauteng where people have experienced development like Diepsloot. Things we didn't have in 1997/8, we have now: two clinics, our kids used to have to go to schools elsewhere and now there are schools here ...'

The problem lay in the way the Alliance partners approached these issues. 'There are issues that are genuine, but they must raise them properly. You can't run away from structures. What kind of ANC members are these? I think it is high time that structures must rule on these things.'

Councillor Ndlazi is even sharper in his criticism of the Alliance partners, as I find when I finally get to meet him. Arrangements have to be made through a frustrated personal assistant, and he misses one meeting before I find him in his office in the municipal library building. Sitting beneath formal photographs of the premier and mayor, and a huge aerial picture of the settlement, he pointedly makes me sit and watch him for a good few minutes while he finishes the work he is doing. He is dressed casually, an ANC cap perched on his head.

Ndlazi is a Diepsloot 'founder': one of the original Zevenfontein squatters, he has been here for 15 years. He wears this history with distinction. 'We were the first people fighting for this land,' he says. 'I started in the ANC in 1981 during school [and when the organisation was still banned] in Witbank. I was in the United Democratic Front in Standard Six. Then I came to Joburg in 1985 and joined the construction industry. In 1987, I formed a union representing people in that construction site, and then I was an administrator for a taxi association for six months.' That is where his detractors' designation of him as a 'taxi driver' must have originated.

He was one of those in Zevenfontein who, tired of waiting for the land to be developed before they could be moved, and sitting on land the Rhema Church had bought for them, packed up their shacks on Easter Monday 1995 and arrived in Diepsloot. 'Our fear was that others would occupy our land. The contractor was not finished, but we just squeezed in.'

In 1998, a city councillor from Soweto passed away and Ndlazi was appointed a 'proportional representation councillor', a councillor who does not represent a ward but is appointed to achieve the right overall proportional representation in the Joburg Council. In 2000, he was reappointed to this position, and then in 2006 he moved to become a ward councillor for one of Diepsloot's two wards in the election where Rogers lost out.

Ndlazi is quick to get to what he sees as the problem of local politics. 'There is this language,' he says. 'We call it power-mongering. There is nothing else. It is only someone who wants to be a chairperson or branch secretary, because you will get a job, you will be able to talk to a developer, you will have access to a councillor to get information for your own benefit.'

This would become worse now that elections were coming up. 'Everyone wants to popularise him or herself to become councillor.'

Asked if he will be standing again, he falls back on protocol: 'If the people still need me, I will stand. We are servants of the people.' That means yes.

His major difficulty is with Sanco. 'It is difficult to work with them,' he says. 'You give them information and they misuse it in the community. You tell them this thing is red, and they call a meeting and say this thing is yellow. They give the wrong side to the community ... they want the impossible. I don't know if the difference is personal, or what. I am not too sure.

'For example, we have an area called Section 6 or 11. It is 6 on the map, but people call it 11. The officials came with a complaint that there was no access to that area [for emergency vehicles]. So I made an inquiry and find that there is an illegal taxi rank at one end and at the other entrance there are illegal shacks. I spoke to Housing to move about 20 shacks to open it up. Sanco organised a March with 1 000 people to make riots because they said we want to move them outside of Diepsloot.

'Whenever we have a project, they oppose it. Whenever someone comes here with a problem, I have to address it, and Sanco says it is wrong, always.

'Even today, people are struggling with access to that area.'

But he is also positive about progress in Diepsloot. 'According to my view, with the areas that I know, Diepsloot development is 90 per cent, it is leading. This is a young township, it is a baby of democracy. There are townships of 40 years and they don't have a clinic. We have two. In Kliptown [another poor area south of Joburg], they still use a bucket system, but we have flushing toilets.

'So in terms of development, it is excellent. Excellent. Ninety per cent.

'Yes, people are living in shacks. We have done more, but there are still challenges. We have only had 14 years and we have built 5 545 RDP houses' – with astounding precision, as if he cast the concrete on each one personally. 'We are lucky. To me, it makes sense.'

Why then the protests? 'It goes back to power-mongering, and misinformation. We said to people we want to move plus-minus 800 shacks to extend the sewer pipe. We had to because there is a big problem with sewage. Sanco tells people we want to move them out of Diepsloot. And they call that [the trouble that erupts] service delivery protests? It is because of Sanco.

'We are spending R11,2-million to upgrade the sewerage and

Sanco says people can't be moved. The reason is that they have sold some of the land and those shacks don't have numbers. And we will see what they have done there if we start to move them.'

It is true that this area has seen significant development within a few years, more than Kliptown but less than Alexandra, which was the focus of a special presidential intervention, the Alex Renewal Programme. There is no lack of visible activity: when I first visit, workers are finishing off the road in Government Precinct, and a few months later it is being torn up for huge stormwater pipes to be put in – suddenly there are piles of stormwater pipes all over the settlement. Then an old rubbish dump on the southern side has bulldozers flattening it one day, and prefab buildings emerge overnight, though no one seems certain what is going up here.

Let's be clear about what has been done and what is being done, as set out for me by each city department and the mayor's office.

So far, 5 280 houses have been built. In addition, the City Department of Housing lists two ongoing and two future plans. Mazotsho Construction has been appointed to build 1 000 units in Extension 4 and 5, of which 170 have been completed and 215 are under construction. An experiment in alternative building technology is underway in Extension 5. One show house has been completed, and the plan is to build 500. This uses a form of construction known as Moladi, in which cement is poured into a framework of crates and steel bars before the crates are removed and reused. It is, apparently, cheap and strong.

The Joburg Property Company has – quite separately – commenced planning for a mixed income development in Diepsloot South, where the Wastewater Treatment Plant is currently located. None of the literature says how many houses will be built, but it is an investment of R1,5-billion and will be 50 per cent

RDP housing, 25 per cent for those in the 'gap market' (those who don't qualify for a free house but also don't earn enough to get a bank bond) and 25 per cent for rental and high-end housing. This will be 'an icon for mixed income development and will be a national and international lesson in social integration'. It is at the stage of concept design.

And then there is Diepsloot East, a provincial project, intended to provide about 5 000 mixed income housing units, two primary schools, two high schools, clinics, churches, business sites and other community facilities. As we have seen, this project has been complicated by the presence of The Frog.

Joburg Water is upgrading the sewer system, which is overloaded and frequently blocked. They are replacing the piping, rehabilitating 171 public toilets and building 300 more at a cost of R13,6-million.

City Power spent R450 000 on public lighting in 2003/4, R1,56-million the following year, and R1,4-million the year after.

City Parks were involved in the Diepsloot Park, an impressive open space, and are spending R250 000 from the Development Bank and R100 000 private donation on a Diepsloot West Park, still under construction. They have also developed two cemeteries.

There are now five government schools – two primary, two intermediate and two secondary, accommodating 7 122 students – a sixth is being built and a seventh planned for the new area of Diepsloot East. There is also one private school, which plays an important role because it is the only one able to take in 'undocumented' students – those born to illegal foreigners – who now live in the area and cannot be accepted into government schools.

There are two clinics, one of which was upgraded in 2010 from eight to eighteen consulting rooms.

And the private sector has played a role too. On the edge of the area is the new Diepsloot Mall, built by a black property developer and a major bank, and sold last year for R128-million. It brings a number of major chain stores to the area, including what is reportedly one of the most successful Shoprite supermarkets in the country. It is a meeting place, a haven, a major community resource.

The Government Precinct at the entrance to the township is an impressive model of municipal construction by any standards – to say, as is often done, that there is no government service delivery would be wrong. The Joburg Development Agency is spending about R30-million from the government's Neighbourhood Development Partnership Grant upgrading this street.

There is no building work going on at the police station on this street, however, and for months I see no progress. I later learn that the builder's funds have been frozen because of a dispute on some other job and they cannot finish this job until their funds are freed up.

It is still hard to credit Diepsloot as a model of development, even in the areas where formal housing has been built: the rock-strewn roads, the overflowing sewage, the overcrowding, the lack of electricity in some areas, the piles of waste, the ram-shackle toilets.

The schools are extremely crowded. At one school, I find groups of up to 60 kids crammed into hot, dark and stuffy converted shipping containers, four or five to a desk, and with an average of a staff member for every 34 learners. At the best school, I am unable to gain access to see how they achieved their 95 per cent pass rate.

The two clinics are neat and businesslike, but also visibly overstretched. You need to get there by 6 am if you want to be seen that day, as they close the gates when they reach their daily quota, and anyone who comes after 7 am is unlikely to be seen, no matter how sick. If women go into labour after hours, or there is an emergency, they have to travel a long distance to the Helen Joseph Hospital, as the clinics close after hours and on weekends.

There are a number of functional and well-kept community halls, which seem to be frequently used. When I ask why there are two within a block of each other, I am told that sometimes a building like this was part of some official's 'KPAs' (Key Performance Assessment criteria) and so they were built whether or not they were needed.

The Development Bank's social needs survey of 2008 recorded that 70 per cent of the houses in Diepsloot were informal, unemployment was 54 per cent, 73 per cent lived below the poverty line and HIV prevalence exceeded 50 per cent. This was early in the recession. The bank calculated the shortfall in social services and – based again on a conservative population figure of 150 000 (probably about a third short of reality) – concluded that just to meet 'contextual' local standards (and not national or international standards), the area needed six more primary schools, four more secondary schools, four more clinics and two community hospitals, seven more libraries, five more community centres, a sports stadium and 20 more sports fields, eight fixed and four mobile post offices, seven police stations and eight mobile stations, two more fire stations and 17 more public open spaces.

The core issue, though, is housing, and that just can't keep pace with the demand as people continue to flow into the area. Diepsloot has taken over the problem of Alex, where housing improvement could never keep up with the ever-increasing numbers, but now they cannot relocate the problem elsewhere. The supply of housing cannot keep up.

So there is a howling dissonance between the progress proclaimed proudly by the councillors and the ANC leadership, and the reality of what one sees there. The politicians are right to say there has been significant development and it is wrong to say that nothing has been done, there is no progress and the ANC government has not improved people's lives. But development has not kept pace with the growth of the place, not nearly. It has made a significant dent in some people's living conditions and a negligible dent in those of most people. To hold up a centre of such poverty, overcrowding and poor conditions as somewhere that has seen more development than most places is a sad, sad indictment. After every interview with the leadership, I walk through the area and am struck by the disjuncture between the progress they proclaim and the reality that presents itself.

CHAPTER FOUR

'I wish I would wake up one morning and find myself in the suburbs'

Musicians often have unusual names and shifting identities, but in this case the name and the person seem to be only loosely connected. Asking around about local artists, I am sent to find a man known as Masimbe'ezinja, which translates as 'dog shit'. But he introduces himself by the name printed on his self-published CDs, *Umasi' ezinja*, meaning 'Sourmilk for dogs'. But then in his songs he uses the former version. It seems he slips between the two.

What I do not expect when I meet the man behind these names is a traditionalist in a security guard's uniform, in his mid-forties. His real name is Michael Nkosi and he has just come off night shift, in the faux-police uniform of a security company. Nkosi is a traditional, self-taught, Zulu musician who performs with half a dozen young women dancers and singers, aged 14–16. His name, he says, was given to him by his audiences.

He takes me to his house, which is fronted by the smallest tavern I have ever seen, run by his wife. Jutting from the stand out onto the street, it is a tiny, roughly built structure just big enough to take a small pool table (if you use short cues). There

is a totem pole of huge speakers to provide music and a hatch
with security bars behind it, from where you can order your
beer. Decor consists only of a few tattered Black Label signs.
Behind the tavern is a small cemented courtyard where he prac-
tises with his dancers.

We sit down to talk in the back of the tavern on seats wedged
between beer fridges.

Nkosi moved from Alexandra to Diepsloot in 2001, but came
originally from a small place in rural KwaZulu-Natal. This
house, he says, is his wife's. His own RDP house is in dispute, as
it was illegally occupied before it was handed over to him. The
authorities have told him they will 'make a plan', and now he
is on standby for another house. It is an interesting example of
one family being in line for two hand-out houses: the move to
Diepsloot was clearly a good investment on their part.

His main instrument is the accordion, but now he picks up a
guitar to strum and launches into song, his voice suddenly high-
pitched, the sound distinctly rural, with the plaintive timbre of
the KZN outdoors.

'This is from God, not from school,' he says. 'I grew up on the
farm, so I am not educated. I am teaching myself.

'Music is my talent: God has given it to me. I don't play an
international sound. It is me, it is from me. No one else can play
this.'

He is called upon to perform at various government events
and functions and gets a big reception. 'But I am blocked,' he
says, 'I need a distributor.' He cannot find a music publisher,
or backing to press more than the few CDs he has around the
house.

'I need a sponsor, I do not have money to distribute.'

Umasi' ezinja sings of his love for voluptuous women ('I want
a Mercedes'), himself ('Mighty eagle' or 'Oh lion, oh lion, mighty
lion'), his rural origins ('I am from Newcastle, at Matsheke-
Tshekeni village, a place built on a small river that quenches my

thirst'), coming home after night-shift ('We will tip-toe because they are sleeping'), a liking for Castle Stout ('Some say it will knock you down, but its taste will'), poverty and politics ('We are hungry, really hungry. It's OK. It's OK. Let's vote for our government'), the dangers of HIV/AIDS ('Hey lady, let's go to the clinic and do a blood test first'), prostitution ('Oh, what has the money done to us?'), Zimbabweans ('We see them here in South Africa every day. Give them their land back') and then, inexplicably, relations between South Africa and Germany ('Hey Germans in Germany ... We would like to meet you').

He has one song that mentions Diepsloot directly, and it speaks about those who burnt facilities during protests:

> *They are boycotting in Diepsloot*
> *They burnt up toilets and government offices*
> *They thought they were giving the government some*
> *   shit*
> *But they were actually shitting on themselves.*
> *I met them the following day.*
> *'I want to go to the toilet, I want to go to the toilet',*
> *   they said.*
> *They had forgotten that they burned the toilets and*
> *   water tanks the previous day.*

When the Global Studio initiative brought architecture, town planning and engineering students from around the world to do volunteer work in Diepsloot for two weeks in 2007, one of the needs they identified was a platform for aspirant artists. The result was the Arts and Culture Network, a non-profit organisation started by Diepsloot artists and now supported by the city to promote creative work among the residents. It was this body that put me on to the musicians and performers of the area.

'Papi' Sathekge, a tall, thin man who came to Diepsloot from Limpopo in 2003, chairs the Network, operating out of a prefabricated provincial government office standing alongside a basketball court in the Methodist Church grounds. 'Diepsloot is seen as a bad place. But we want to show there are a lot of things happening here, so that in five years, Diepsloot will be a place to come to, rather than people hating and fearing it.' It sounds idealistic, but it reflects his passion for culture.

The Network raises funding and helps the artists find platforms and market themselves. One spring day, they come out to fix, clean and paint Diepsloot's communal toilets, a way to bring people in to see Global Studio's projects and hopefully raise some money. 'We want to spread a message to get people to look after the toilets,' Papi says. 'To love the toilets, we want to say, is to love yourself.' A more down-to-earth use of a toilet than Marcel Duchamp's.

Like many city workers, Kaiser Kubheka has become passionate about what needs to and can be done in Diepsloot. But he admits that his initial reaction when he was posted here was nervousness. He appears at first as a standard grey bureaucrat, but it becomes clear that he has found his métier in arts and culture, and is working steadily through the slow processes of bringing city resources to the artists of Diepsloot. 'It was an unpredictable area. Many of us were scared to go and work there.' Originally, he was sent in by the Sports and Recreation Department, but he saw the need in arts and culture, and used his own time to get involved. He was working on Africa Day celebrations for the city when approached by Global Studio and they teamed up. 'I saw that there was talent, but it needs to be nurtured. We saw a need to unite artists because then – even now – they were difficult to work with because they are so disorganised.'

Out of this grew the Network: Kubheka is now helping them with their registration, tax status and fundraising.

The issue in the beginning was the political leadership of the area. 'It was difficult to distinguish between many leaders and the criminal elements,' he says. 'Diepsloot has been like a varsity to me, because of the difficulties I went through, the challenges I had to deal with and what I had to learn. The very first day I went there, some of the so-called community leaders were not happy about my appointment and I had to survive a life-threatening situation.'

One of his tasks was to supervise the municipal facilities in Diepsloot. 'There was actually no personnel looking after it, so what I discovered about these facilities was the leadership were using it for their own storage garages. I put an end to that, so it was difficult to make friends. People were threatened.'

But things have since settled down. 'Today I am one of them, I have become one of them by understanding the situation and realising I was not just coming to work there, but to contribute to the community. I saw I was better off, but not better than, the people of Diepsloot.

'I realised I was an outsider, so I was trying my best to go on weekends and socialise. So they saw I was not there to bulldoze them or anything, but I was one of them. That brought me closer to them. Also, my work with the Arts and Culture Network, because there was no other official who had a passion for arts and culture – that made me to be recognised.

'They taught me to never say never. And they taught me the little you got, you must be thankful for, because there are always others with less. It has been really nice. I really love it now.'

Kaiser has drawn up a 12-month plan to develop arts and culture in the area, but is waiting for funding to come through. 'We are ready and waiting for the city to help implement.'

From the local rappers, I get a very different insight into being young in this place. Diep Movement is made up of three hip-hop artists who hold regular weekend sessions with about 50 local kids.

'We do session at parties. And every Sunday, we have an open session where we do freestyle and we encourage the youngsters to do tracks,' says Tony Ntsimane. 'We are trying to take them off the streets. There are lots of bad things happening with the youth. There are lots of drugs. The new one and the worst one is tik, or taiwan, they call it, or *ngope*.

'We give them a message: don't do drugs. We teach them about diseases like Aids, and rather get them to come to arts and culture to keep busy. I walk around and see lots of youths hanging around. I plan to also do some entertaining or arts classes, maybe drama, during the day.'

His colleagues work. 'I am the only one unemployed, I have just got a little business, making ices for the kids.'

Tony lives in Extension 7, in a shack in a yard, rented for about R350 per month, with power and water. He has lived in Diepsloot for three years, 'but the kids all know me because my mother is a teacher at Fourways.'

'To live here, it is okay,' he says. 'I would not want to get out and go to Soweto or Alex. A lot of entertainment is happening there and here at least I can leave a mark behind, because there is no entertainment here.

'It is a *kwaai* place.'

Every Monday, there is a *mogadiwa* (a tripe feast) which rotates between the taverns, and they call Diep Movement to play there. People get *pap* and *mogadi* for R25 or R30, a beer for R5 – and some hip hop.

Every now and then they do a full-weekend, three-day session – from Friday afternoon through to Sunday night. 'We do it usually in an unfinished house. We were going to do it last weekend, but decided to leave it to the end of the month [when people have cash].

'We listen to a lot of underground. Commercial stuff, we listen to as well, but not a lot. It is all about money, about getting rich, about bling bling. We rap about how we live, how we grow up.

'At sessions, people sometimes want us to do reggae and

we do it. And we know house and how to use it, but it is not our music. Our music is hip hop. It is about our lives here in Diepsloot.'

The CD they give me has a range of their rappers doing material. They deal with some of the standard issues you would expect: love and desire (the mesmerising 16-year-old who won't go out with the rapper because he does not have money or a flashy car) and their dangers ('You acting as though you don't know [Aids], black people, until when will you choose to die like this? Dying of sex').

One raps about trying not to follow in the footsteps of an absent father:

Father I have a question
I don't want to be like you
My mother told me you don't like questions
Did you hate me or you were scared of your
responsibility?

But many of them have a harder, violent edge as they grapple with the realities of Diepsloot life:

I wish I would wake up one morning
And find myself in the suburbs
Dressed like a king
My wife with a ring on a finger
Burning the Devil's skull
Turning him into ashes
But now every time I wake up
I feel like I'm in the forest
My eyes can't see clearly
The Devil is here, taking people out of the way
Leading them into danger
Let's stand up in the townships
Let's stop the nonsense and take care of ourselves

The singer then tells of going drinking – 'I forget that the money I am using brings food on the table' – and in search of women: 'I am up and down, looking for women, to help me misuse this money that I got.'

He decides 'on the spot' to go to the shopping suburb of Rosebank where he 'smashes up things' and 'take[s] the missus' purse'.

> As time went by life became rough
> I started to think again about being a gangster
> There is no other way, I'll go and rob
> Jumping fences,
> I'm under the influence of drugs

He describes hijacking a BMW and having nightmares about it:

> This man almost had an accident with his Beemer
> He applied brakes and his wife is a fool
> I pulled my gun and told myself I'm killing them
> I felt the devil calling my name
> I opened the door and pulled the trigger
> I put them inside the boot and I drove off
> Now I have nightmares every day
> I regret what the works of the pistol do

Another song glorifies the rituals of a gangster funeral:

> Gunshots everywhere, parents are scared
> It is not like the olden days anymore
> People wear short-skirts at the graveside
> The youth of today does things differently
> Traditional days are no more
> Smoking dagga all over the place, not forgetting alcohol
> After-tears, this is how we roll
> Ladies are beautiful
> The burial is over, we wash our hands
> We have accompanied him

... We don't care; we are drinking from the bottle
Spinning the car, the smoke is all around us
Everything is good and in order
It's nice, we are enjoying this
We all have lost a loved one
No disrespect, today the beat is on high
We'll be doing this till the morning comes

And the chorus:
After-tears, we dance and dance
After-tears, we party and party
We drink and drink
We party
After-tears

Another sings of the battle to grow up when one is engulfed by
problems:
There is no future in this land
People are unemployed, poverty is stubborn
Death attacks anyone
In the ghetto I hear gunshot echoes
In Soweto, Diepkloof, Diepsloot, Alexandra, etc
These townships are all the same
The gangsters stab and shoot one another
There is no peace, there is no peace
Even though things are like this, I still grow
Even though things are like this, I still sing

They rap about the violence of their everyday lives:
We were chilling and drinking
Some guys came and started a fight with us
Breaking bottles, whipping them, they left in blood
We thought it was over but we were wrong
They came back with guns

They didn't waste time, they opened gunshots
My friend died on the spot
Police were too late
The body was still when the ambulance got there
The body was cold and the breath no more
Death kept on following me but God has kept me
  alive
I keep on surviving
I guess my ancestors are watching over me
But since that day I have sleepless nights
I don't know a good sleep anymore
In fact there is no sleep at all.

It is stark, chilling imagery of life in a violent hood: 'The body was cold and the breath no more'. Death is quick and close; survival is due only to good fortune. There is no escaping these tough realities. 'I don't know a good sleep anymore.'

CHAPTER FIVE

'I can't vote for you if you are not helping me'

It is a gusty, chilly winter morning; Francinah Mbaduli brushes off two chairs for us to sit and talk in the dusty open space outside the shack that serves as the Sanco office in Diepsloot. The dark inside of the shack – no electricity, no flooring, nothing in it but a mixture of old and broken chairs – is too cold, she says. The windows are smashed and partly boarded up with broken bits of wood. 'Let's sit in the sun.' Every now and then we are smothered in smoke from a smouldering dumpster on the side of the street and she is irritated: 'They are not supposed to do that,' she says, summoning two men wearing the uniform of the street cleaners, Pikitup, to discuss it.

The ANC leadership I have been speaking to see their 'allies' in Sanco as the source of their difficulties. They accuse Sanco of running a mob-like organisation, taking protection money from locals, threatening foreigners, and selling access to the land and shacks.

All agree that Sanco has a hold on the cluster of informal shacks known as the Reception Area; that their chair, known only as Letsoalo, is a man of considerable power, and Francinah is his side-kick. Just meeting with her in this place is in stark contrast to meeting with the ANC leadership, who use the

73

municipal offices as their own. It makes tangible her and her colleagues' exclusion from the circles of official power and resources.

As always, the streets are teeming with people, many of them greeting her. While we are talking, people come up to ask her help. A man named Amos shows a receipt from a nearby shop where he left a car battery to be charged the previous day. When he went back today, the battery was not there. Francinah tells him she will take it to the block coordinator, who will take it up with the owner of the shop. 'But, please, don't fight,' she says to him, changing to English for my benefit. 'We don't want fighting.' When he leaves, I ask if she gets lots of these requests for help. 'Too many,' she laughs. 'But they don't always find me here. That is why I am running away sometimes.' She pauses and adds: 'But it is good that they know they have somewhere to come to to sort these things out.'

Francinah is secretary of Sanco for Ward 95 and has lived here since 1996, when she was sent to Diepsloot by the city government to work on shack and land allocation. 'I was staying at the American School, where my husband was working, and I was working for the city. There was nothing here,' she says, indicating with a sweep of her hand the area we are in. 'There were only a few shacks called the Rhema shacks, because the people had gone to Rhema Church in Randburg when they were thrown off their land and then they were brought here.

'I was one of those who helped allocate the shacks. Then I came to live here. I was a founder of Sanco, and I was an ANC member, and I am deputy chair of the SACP for this ward. I did that [housing] work until the time came – I think it was 1999 – to build RDP housing. Our contract ended in 1998 and then the city took over allocating the houses. Then they took me to city finance, where I dealt with funding for the RDP houses.'

She points at the shacks. 'These places are supposed to be empty. These are new people. They built houses for those first people and they were supposed to be finished, but then they brought the Alex people. Now there is a new waiting list for houses.'

Francinah resigned from the city a year ago and started her own company, doing security in Honeydew – 'and still looking for other jobs' – as well as construction in Pretoria. I asked if her company did work in Diepsloot, whether she was one of the many queuing for tenders here. 'There is no work here, but even if there is, everyone is fighting for those jobs, so I decided let's not be in those fights. Let's go elsewhere.'

In February, she was elected to the Sanco ward executive as treasurer and sees herself as a reformer. 'I came here because I didn't want people to toyi-toyi so much. We thought we should be in the community to tell them what is going on and what they should do. We are trying to give information to the community and to lead them. So now there has been no toyi-toying since February.

'There was supposed to be these xenophobic attacks now [following the World Cup], so we called a meeting on Saturday. Lots of people were here, they came here,' she says, gesturing again around the empty space. 'It was a very big meeting, and we told the people we did not want these attacks.'

Has development been slow? 'It has been a bit slow, but now there are promises to put more houses in Diepsloot East. It was supposed to start in May or June [2010], so we are waiting, but they are busy, they can start any time.' This is optimistic, as this development – the crucial next step for Diepsloot – is not expected to start for some time yet. Everyone gives me a different time scale.

Francinah tells me a story about people who invaded some new houses which were waiting to be allocated. 'They [the authorities] tried to take them out, there was lots of toyi-toying, but they are still in there. There was a lot of fighting.'

The problem was one of leadership, she says, and this sets her off. 'They [the political and city leadership] are not guiding the people to say what they can or cannot do. Especially the ANC leaders, they do nothing, they are only involved in the development projects and only their contractors get the jobs.'

Is she not an ANC member? 'Yes, but the chairperson is different. They run the projects and don't involve anyone, they work only with the councillors.'

She presents a picture of an ANC leadership that occupies official structures and operates at the level of project management, working out of the city and other formal offices, handing out work to their families and friends. In contrast, Sanco is on the ground, working and interacting with people, organising on the streets, operating out of this small shack in Extension 1.

How many members does Sanco have? 'Everyone is a member, I can say that half this community is a Sanco member. They pay R20 for a two-year membership.'

She denies strongly that shops and business are made to pay Sanco.

Much of her dissatisfaction is aimed at the city leadership. 'The roads are bad, but the city will tell you they have no budget.

'There is a lot of unemployment here. I used to take peoples' CVs to the city – but they don't like people from Diepsloot, only from Soweto. Even the city offices here, the people in them are from outside. They don't employ our people here. Maybe if they did, people would come out of their shacks. I am blaming the city. People need jobs, then they will be able to buy a nice house.'

I asked her what she thought of the coming local elections. 'The fighting has already started, people are fighting for these positions. It is nice to be a councillor, but you have to deliver. It is useless if you just want to be a councillor for the money.

'There is lots of division, terrible fighting, between ANC members. There are two groups in the ANC now, one is with the chair of the ANC and one with the secretary. It is these ones

– who are with the secretary – who are the powerful ones. It is all about who you support and who is doing good for you. With the chair, he just grabs the jobs for himself and does not help people here; the secretary is involved in building the police station, and he hired people from the community. People are seeing this and they will vote for the ones doing good for the community. I can't vote for you if you are not helping me.'

She is dismissive of Rogers, the ANC chair. 'He doesn't care about people,' she says. Councillor Isaac Maele is 'all right'. He is trying to reconnect with people and rebuild relations. The other councillor isn't worth talking about, she says, waving her hand dismissively.

Was it true that Sanco was behind the service delivery protests? 'It was Sanco who did this, but it was the old Sanco, not the new Sanco. There won't be protests if we show people what is happening.'

She tells me a story of how the new Sanco operates. 'In April, there was no water for three weeks, people wanted to toyi-toyi. We called together the councillors and the community, we called Joburg Water, we told them people are angry. They told us of the burst pipe and told us what they were doing to fix it. We gave them five hours to repair it, or we would toyi-toyi. That afternoon we had water.

'They did it same day because they could see the people were angry. Even the councillor [Maele] was digging the ground,' she chuckles. 'He was helping with a spade.'

'I didn't like the old Sanco. Me and Mr Letsoalo said this is not right the way things were happening. On March 29, we had a march for people who were evicted in Dainfern. They wanted to march but I said it must be legal. We applied, we got permission, we marched there and back and there was no problem. It was so nice.

'I believe in negotiating, but not fighting. If you talk to people, if you come down to their level, then they see you are part of the same community, and they will listen.'

She is contemptuous of Minister Tokyo Sexwale and his high-profile visit to the area. 'Tokyo just came and stayed a night and nothing happened. He saw some areas that were so dirty, with sewage running in the street, he saw it and said something must be done. He came and stayed, but there was no delivery.

'People are becoming impatient. It is only because we are addressing them, saying that something is coming, wait, be patient ...' There is an implicit threat in this: if Sanco stops saying this, things will blow up.

I go in search of representatives of other political parties: the Democratic Alliance and the Inkatha Freedom Party. Neither has a visible presence in the area and all of them have to be tracked down through their national party structures. In the 1996 elections, the ANC won well over 90 per cent of all the Diepsloot votes, losing to the DA only in two voting stations in the surrounding, wealthier areas. In Diepsloot itself, the IFP won in the region of 4 per cent and the DA about half that. About 30 per cent of registered voters bothered to cast their ballot, which was not exceptional but indicates a low level of engagement in an area where the council has so much to deliver and the councillors' positions are so contested.

Through the DA's city council leadership, I locate the party's regional office and am told that their person in Diepsloot is Irene Mathebula.

Irene's real name is Refilwe; she invites me to her place in Extension 2, where her family has had a stand since 1995. They live in a cluster of shacks, awaiting fulfilment of a promised RDP house. 'We applied and it was approved, but we don't know why it has not been built,' she says.

Meanwhile, there are 11 of them in the family compound – her parents, siblings and their children and her own young son. None of them are working at the moment, except doing part-time jobs 'just to survive'. Her father, who was the last employed family member, recently lost his job. Irene was last employed in marketing four years ago, and now just has one or two clients for whom she does occasional jobs. The family gets grants for four of the young children. 'We are just trying to survive. It is still hard,' she says. She is in her early thirties.

Irene has a stylishness and glamour, dressed in a tight skirt and stiletto heels which demand some courage on the rough roads of Diepsloot. We chat in her shack, which is small and packed with feminine things, the intense living space of a proud young woman, all make-up and mirrors and clothing and soft dolls. Later we walk through the area, though it is hard to talk because she is greeting and chatting to everyone on the way, and she takes me to the nearby school, where she is chair of the governing body (SGB).

Irene's affiliation with the DA is built around the opportunities it holds out for her. She grew up in a staunch ANC family, but is disillusioned with the local leadership. 'I achieved nothing there. If you don't have a friend in the right places in the ANC, you will not have anything. They don't recognise you, they only use you.'

The local councillor is no help. 'He doesn't even know our school. He does not know our SGB. He never comes to meetings.'

'These councillors are too slow in dealing with things and attending to matters, especially if you look at our living environment. They told us the toilets here were temporary, but they have been temporary now for more than 10 years. There are no houses and we don't know the reasons. They say the money is not there, it has vanished. I am not impressed with their leadership.'

Through her work for the school, she met Michael Sun, the regional DA leader, and he brought her into the party. 'With the DA all the opportunities are there. If you call them, MPs or anyone, they come and meet with us here. They have time for me.' Sun had helped the school with books, and with their 'One learner, one chair' campaign to ensure that every pupil at least had somewhere to sit.

Many Diepsloot people are disillusioned with the ANC, she says, but scared to come out for the DA, saying it is a white party. 'That's bullshit,' she says. 'I think I am going far with the DA. I have been networking myself. I am interested in being an entrepreneur, and I am going to meet someone who is going to help me there.'

When I find the IFP's Simon Mabaso, he says the reason the DA is weak in Diepsloot is because he left and took most of their members to the IFP. Mabaso is now the IFP chair, but was the DA chair until 2006. 'I was Ward 96 candidate for DA and was chair of the DA here. I was a member of the federal council, and I was on their PR (proportional representation) list as well. But after the election I did not go in on the PR list. The DA took another person and didn't tell me. It was a problem.'

I met Mabaso in his RDP house, which he has expanded to cover almost the whole stand with three or four buildings for his family and for rental. He is himself a builder, owner of Thambiso Building Construction CC, and drives a bakkie which offers 'Building, plastering, painting, tiling …' But times are tight. 'I am not busy now. This World Cup has made us suffer,' he says.

'I can't be ANC, because it is too much [like] the mafia. They don't tell people the truth, they make lies all the time.

'The councillors are not delivering. Everything is poor. There are no houses, and the roads are very bad. This councillor is too much [involved] in corruption. If I can tell you about a project, it is just his friends. If you are not family of the councillor, then you can't get nothing. If I am not the brother of someone in the ANC office, I can't get a house. I have people who have been waiting since 1996 for a house, and they are still staying in the squatter camp. I have been fighting for too long.'

Why do people support the ANC? I ask. 'Sometimes people are blind. At election time, the ANC starts to make promises and bribe people. They tell them there are no [government] grants if they don't vote ANC.'

The ANC tries to control everything, he says, but they know him and leave him alone. 'They don't come and disturb me.

'The IFP now has too many members, because I brought DA members to the IFP. There is about 350 members in Ward 96 and more than 270 in Ward 95.'

But, he says, there is too much toyi-toying and it is not the opposition parties who are responsible for this. 'The toyi-toying began because of the ANC's election promises. It is ANC people who are toyi-toying.'

It is clear to me that meeting Isaac Maele – the councillor who is drawing the anger of the other ANC leaders and being praised by Sanco – is going to be different. I have a mental picture of him picking up a spade to help dig for burst pipes. Meeting him is difficult, because he is busy. When I arrive I have to wait 20 minutes while he sorts out a problem on his phone, and then he sits down with me in my car for a quick, snatched conversation.

'According to me, [service delivery] is moving too fast. But still much more needs to be done. It is moving, though people are impatient.'

Does this worry him? 'Yes, when people are not happy there will always be trouble. Unemployment is the problem, because where there is unemployment, there is always trouble.'

He shares the view that the previous year's protests were not the acceptable way to pursue things. 'When there were service delivery protests, some of these issues were not correct as they were raised.' But the problem was not lack of delivery, but lack of information: 'Those who were protesting were saying the information was lacking, they were not informed properly. They were frustrated because they had no information, there was a problem with leaders not giving them information. They are unemployed, and they felt they were excluded from the projects that we brought in. They are saying we are not part and parcel of the economic processes where there are benefits for the community.'

Isaac's response is to get down among the people. 'I realise as a leader that we must close that gap. From now on, people will be much more informed. It was an oversight, because when we call a public meeting there are a few hundred people there and we think people are then informed.'

Most of the ANC leaders I speak to are critical of their Alliance partners, but argue that they have to 'engage' with them. Isaac is the only one I see actually doing this: 'Alliance partners felt they were not much recognised and not taken seriously by the ruling party. So we said, let's involve them, let's work together as partners. It is better now, those protests were an opportunity.

'As ward councillor, I single-handedly engaged all the stakeholders. From now on, because I represent everyone as the councillor, you will be informed of everything, I told them. That is why we have not had protests since last year.'

He cites Letsoalo as a key figure. 'He is someone who is much more influential in the community, especially in Extension 1. When he calls a meeting, people listen to him.

'So I put things aside to work with him. You can't say, but he was leading protests, he is negative. Nothing will come of that attitude. He is influential, but he is also a somebody who will listen. I find it interesting to work with him.'

Maybe this is why the other ANC leaders see Maele as having crossed over, as being on 'the other side'.

One of the issues is that Ward Committees, which are a key part of the participatory government model at work here, barely operate. A few years ago, areas like Diepsloot had a Community Development Forum, where these issues were canvassed. They gave way to the creation of Ward Committees, more formal bodies – written into local government laws – which the Ward Councillor is obliged to consult on these matters. They have 'a critical role to play', the Minister for Provincial and Local Government, Sydney Mufamadi, said in a handbook produced for members of these committees in 2005. 'Being a representative structure of the community and citizens, they need to inform the municipality about the aspirations, potentials and problems of the people. They should form a bridge by facilitating proper communication between councils and the citizens they represent.'

Not in Diepsloot, where they appear to exist in name only. Perhaps it is because they are built on a notion of community which does not reflect reality. Sanco's Francinah is contemptuous of these committees because the ANC is too divided to manage them. Maele puts it down to more basic issues: 'My Ward Committee operates, but it is not efficient. The issue is that sometimes people get motivated around the stipend or remuneration. People are not interested otherwise. They currently get R50 per meeting, which is not enough because they also need to travel.'

Maele dismisses suggestions that anyone is giving tenders and contracts to their friends and cadres. 'The issue of tenders is not our competency at the local level. The government department does that, and when they come here, they have already appointed the contractor and when the contractor comes here he will have to work with local sub-contractors. As Ward Councillors, we cannot interfere.

'The main contractor must decide who to work with, otherwise when they don't deliver, they will say it was because we interfered. We don't want that – when someone fails, he must fail by himself.

'Jobs for pals? I will not say it is not happening in some areas, but here it is transparent. There is a process of interviews, advertisements. There are those who prefer their candidates and want to get them in, but we will not allow them. We want each one to go through the processes.'

The phone rings, and Maele has to run off.

I find the SA Communist Party by peering at a tiny notice stuck on the door of a community centre, calling for a meeting of the Zola Zemba Branch of Ward 96 and giving the number of branch secretary Sam Seale. I arrange to meet Sam; he has an emergency and reschedules. When we meet again he tells me that protocol requires me first to call the regional secretary. I do so, am given the okay and sit down with Sam in the shack which serves as the Community Police Forum offices.

The SACP is strong in Diepsloot, he says; his branch has about 200 members. 'We are lucky for our branch to be named after a hero' – Zola Zemba, he tells me, was an MK fighter who lived in the Indian township of Lenasia and was shot dead during apartheid. In fact, an internet search tells me that Zemba was the *nom de guerre* of Archie Sibeko, a trade unionist and former ANC camp commander who recently turned up very much alive to receive the Presidential Order of Luthuli in Silver for his struggle service.

Asked about relations with the Alliance partners, Sam starts by making it clear that he is a walking embodiment of the ruling Alliance in all its local formations: 'I am a member of the ANC, an executive on the Sanco branch, secretary of the Communist Party branch and sit on the Community Policing Forum.' How he weaves together these roles is crucial to understanding the role he is playing in this area.

Alliance relationships are terrible, Sam says, because of the ANC's hostility to communists. 'We are of the view that from the time we launched the party here, the ANC was against us, saying we can't launch here. They didn't want communists. They say we are the opposition, but we are not. We want the Alliance to be alive.'

They have never had an Alliance meeting in the area. 'We wrote so many times to them, and they did not answer us. We also talked to the ANC chair.'

As to Sanco, Sam makes it clear that there are two Sancos in Diepsloot, one in each ward, and he has little respect for the one led by Francinah. It is not sufficient that each organisation is fighting the others; each organisation is also fighting with itself.

The problem, he says, is leadership. 'There is no leadership now. There are only individuals doing their own thing. What I can say is that the community comes first in all what we do. On that side, there is no leadership.' And corruption: 'We work collectively, we expose the corruption of the councillor, like the sale of a permanent stand, or the sale of RDP houses. As a party, we cannot take corruption.'

While development is happening, it is too tightly controlled by what he calls the 'fake leadership'. 'Development is still in the hands of the councillor. They still own all the projects. If you are not his friend, you cannot get a job.'

Councillor Maele is 'feeling the heat'. 'He wants a second term, but he is taking a chance. He must end his term and leave and the community will choose their leader.' Sam has even greater contempt for the other councillor, Ndlazi: 'We won't support him again. He doesn't know what he is doing. If you lack knowledge, you have to go back to school. You have to be a councillor of the community, not a councillor of the office. You have to walk around here.'

The service delivery protest of last year was a turning point in Alliance relations. 'We are the ones who protested against the council. We had an agreement that we would march peacefully, we had permission, but our comrades were arrested, I myself was arrested, but I was not taken to court.

'We don't protest now, because they are listening to what we are saying. We were not accusing anyone, we were telling of real things. We said you must open your eyes or resign. Now they are listening. The fact is that they came to us, we showed them what the community was saying, they were sitting in their office and did not know, they could not even meet with the community.'

The coming local government elections will be critical, and the SACP is developing a clear plan to seize control: 'The ward and the proportional representation councillors will come from the [Communist] Party. We are going to make sure the candidates are from the Party. In Ward 96, we are in good standing, we can take back the ANC as the Party. We sit with our own members and we discuss who to vote for, everyone will then go and vote in the ANC.'

The fight for the control of the soul of the ANC that is being played out on the national platform is mirrored at a local, branch level. It is a battle for control of the local structures, and it is rough and tough. It is not dressed up in ideological language, but presented as a fight for access to the city's resources.

Perhaps the clearest view I get of these battles came from another outsider, activist-researcher Kindiza Ngubeni, of the Centre for the Study of Violence and Reconciliation. I visit him in his small, sparse office in Braamfontein for an outpouring of his dark view of the politics of Diepsloot, picked up while researching the area and convening Community Dialogues for the Nelson Mandela Foundation. The Foundation has tried to get internal communication forums going in the areas most affected by xenophobic violence and 'service delivery' protests. When the first such meeting on Diepsloot made little progress, he had to go out and do more groundwork, find out what were the dynamics they were missing. He dipped into a deep cauldron of rivalry and intrigue.

Diepsloot, he says, is a place of organised chaos, a result of the haphazard way in which it was established. 'It was not well planned; it came about because of pressure from the first group that came there from Zevenfontein. That is where things started, because there was a struggle for ownership of the place.

'From that stage, the problem was that the government did not build a police station, and that was bound to mean there would be chaos without such an institution. The formation of Sanco was dominated by the Zevenfontein group, but then the second lot came from Honeydew and Randburg and later Alex – these were displaced families who were invading land. The first group were put there [in the Resettlement Area] as a temporary measure, and people were documented. Then the place was swelling, and it became no longer just a resettlement area, a transit area.'

What Kindiza describes as 'the Zevenfontein structures' established control in the absence of formal institutions and determined who came in and under what terms. 'Sanco became the law in Diepsloot. They started establishing community courts and street committees. As the place developed, the government could not cope and it became a dumping ground. Whenever land was needed, people were taken to Diepsloot. It ballooned, and now there are over 150 000 people there.

'So there is chaos, no infrastructure, some streets are so tiny you can't get through. Even now there is only a mobile police station with two cars in the area and people who had serious cases had to go to Erasmia, 10 km away.

'Sanco exploited that. They did their own policing, and that is where corruption and exploitation came in. People had to pay R50 for their case to be heard [by the community court] and that opened a door for corruption. People began to buy their way out.

'When the police came, Sanco said we are not going to be dictated to by the police, they have to report and get access via Sanco.

'As the government built RDP houses, and bought more land for these houses, more people were dumped in the Reception

Area. People were being relocated, but as Diepsloot expanded, the Reception Area was still growing. People were realising the potential to get land and came from all around.

'The Civic [Sanco] was controlling the Reception Area. As people were moved out into RDP houses, they sold the land and the shacks to new people. And now these people had no documentation, they sold also to foreign nationals.

'This continued until the [City] Housing Department established an office there and people were told to register their shacks to get an RDP house. As people were registering, people who owed allegiance to Sanco, people would come to ask for land to build a shack. I saw it myself, people came into the Sanco office, ask, pay and get land ... all the shopkeepers pay monthly to Sanco for protection.

'In essence, we realised that our [Nelson Mandela Foundation] dialogues were premised on weak foundations. We had not done enough groundwork to establish who were the stakeholders. We were quick to bring people together and had the wrong people there, so we did not achieve our goals. The majority of participants were from the Community Development Forum [the formal and official consultation body] and actual stakeholders like the Community Policing Forum, Sanco and the street committees were not there.'

It is a lesson on the parallel, informal structures which have real influence. 'The ANC is not on the ground. There you find the SACP, the Civic, the SACP Youth League – these are the ones on the ground. The ANC is preoccupied with government projects, and they are most of the people involved in these projects or they are the contractors to do these projects. So the SACP and Sanco are left out, that is why they want to rock the government. They leak information to the people on the ground.

'There is bitterness towards those who benefit from projects. There are two wards and two councillors, but the most problematic is Ward 95. It is uncontrollable and runs the whole of

Diepsloot because the Reception Area is there. It is like a mafia who runs it, and now people say they have Zimbabwean war veterans who are giving protection there.

'Police can't penetrate the area, so all the people running from the police from the whole area flee there. People there are armed to the teeth. People think they are ex-Zim combatants because they are trained. Some Sanco members use them as bodyguards.

'I get an SMS one day saying, "We know who you are talking to. We told you there are some people you should not be talking to." They say that after 7 pm, it is a jungle, it is not safe to go there.

'There is so much corruption. You find a Community Policing Forum person is a project director, another is involved in building construction. I met the IFP guy and he kept saying there is no place like this, he is happy to live here. He supported the councillor in Ward 96. Why? I discovered that this guy also is running a construction business and is benefiting from an RDP project. He has extended his RDP house into a big house, and he also has a house in Mpumalanga.'

Local political divisions run deep, and at the centre is a battle for control over development projects and the resources made available by the state. Politics in Diepsloot is not at all comradely, it is fractious. The main fissure is between those in state and party structures – intertwined – who control the available developmental resources and who tend to have state jobs and RDP houses, and those who represent or control the people of the shacks, the unemployed, the marginal of the marginal. Those in the official, formal spaces view their opponents as opportunists, stirring up the uneducated and impatient for their own gain, making their livelihoods through the control of the informal areas. Those in the informal spaces view their opponents as having grown distant from their roots, using their access to power and resources for personal and political gain. It is a battle between formal and informal structures, between those who counsel patience because the ANC will deliver, and those who are sceptical that they will or can without the pressure from below.

Both sides wield power, but from different sources. The insider group has the power of the state, party machinery and the law, while the outsider group has the power of mass mobilisation, clearly a formidable factor in this volatile settlement. They can mobilise the toyi-toyi, or at least threaten it, and close the streets, and the formal leaders implicitly acknowledge this power.

The dislike and distrust of each other is visceral. Yet they remain Alliance partners, are locked together in these structures, and almost all the leaders wear multiple hats. They see the need to engage with each other, but only with the purpose of wresting control of each other's power bases. The divisions run both between and within organisations in the Alliance, and they are personal, bitter and ugly.

These political relationships go through waves of hostility and cooperation. When I started in Diepsloot in mid-2010, the leaders and officials of the Alliance partners talked of each other with open contempt and hostility. By early 2011, when all the players were deeply immersed in choosing candidates for the upcoming local government elections, they were forced together by circumstances and structures. Part of this reflected changes of attitude in ANC national leadership, who under Zuma were now working closer with their Alliance partners, unlike Mbeki, who held them in contempt. On a local level, the ANC needed to work with their partners if they were to avoid a recurrence of the violent eruptions of 2009. And they needed each other for the local government elections, and had to work together in the process to identify and agree on candidates. But the rivalry and tension lurked just below the surface.

Abraham Mabuke, who held office in both the ANC and

SACP branches and who emerged as a candidate himself, said he had taken part in protests in 2010 because at the time the ANC and SACP were not on good terms. He finds it important to assert that the protests were legal and therefore legitimate, partly because participation in illegal toyi-toying might lead to his exclusion as a candidate.

Before the protests, he says, the city council was not 'giving the opportunity for the SACP to engage in the issues [and this] left us no option but to apply for permission to hold a legal protest. I can say that after July 2010 everything changed through the intervention of higher structures, creating an opening for us to engage. So for the first time in the history of this area, the ANC and Alliance structures are working hand in hand.'

There was little doubt among all of those involved, though, that this truce was a temporary one. 'That is politics,' Mabuke says. 'There are no permanent friends, there are no permanent enemies. We agree today and agree to disagree tomorrow. We hope for a long relationship, based on robust engagement, but can't rule out the possibility of some strong disagreements.'

They are united under the banner of the national democratic revolution, but locked in combat because the SACP wants to shift the ANC to the left. The SACP and Sanco's strength lies in the poor majority of Diepsloot, those in shacks, while the ANC tries to represent everyone in Diepsloot and is also locked in close relationships with business and the state. The dividing lines, though, are not always clear. Mabuke describes himself as an entrepreneur: he owns a tavern and a large tuck shop, and has a construction business, though it is dormant because, as he puts it, 'I don't have any tenders at the moment.' He is also employed as a community liaison officer for the building of the police station.

The distance between the allies is apparent in where they operate from and the language they use. I met the ANC leadership in city offices, where they have assistants and telephones and easy access to the city infrastructure. On the other hand, SACP and Sanco offices are dark and empty shacks with a few broken chairs and tables in them, but no electricity and a notable absence of resources. The ANC leadership talks the language of government – it is about following due process, doing things in the proper way, respecting the institutions of the state, the rule of law, being patient about service delivery. The Sanco and SACP leadership speak the language of protest and socialism. They say the ANC leadership spends its time in the city, is not on the streets, is out of touch with the people of Diepsloot and – most important of all – that they keep the jobs and tenders for their families and friends. Indeed, the ANC leadership is employed either by the city or the premier's office or is doing community liaison work on one of the city or provincial building projects. The SACP and Sanco leadership have made their living through their control of the Reception Area and of access to land and shacks there. The Reception Area, home to the bulk of the population, and the Community Policing Forum in each ward are their territory.

The central battle is over political office, but it often feels like this is less an ideological divide than a scrap over access to power and resources. The councillor is seen to have control over development projects, tenders and posts. The councillor appears to have little influence over the city, being just one of several hundred council members, but he does have access to some resources in an area without much to offer, and this puts him at the centre of a system of local patronage. The councillors have city and state resources that give them offices, staff and access to the corridors of power, and influence over who gets jobs, tenders and houses.

To become a councillor, you need to jump through two hoops, each held by one side of the political divide. You have to get a popular vote at branch level, and you have to pass an ANC scrutiny process. At the previous election, two candidates – including Rogers – passed through the first hoop and fell at the second. The balancing act appears to be near-impossible: to win popularity, you have to say and do things that alienate your colleagues who hold the second hoop; to make sure you get through the second, you have to behave in a way that is likely to make it difficult to get through the first. If you get through both, then you are in exactly the same position as those who preceded you: you have some patronage to distribute, but not a lot of influence over the city and the crucial issues of service delivery. You have limited capacity to deliver, or effect delivery.

There is an elaborate candidate selection process which takes many weeks, with the branch making nominations which have to consist of two males and two females, a screening committee representing the full Alliance inspecting their CVs and inter- viewing them, a public meeting in which they are presented and questioned (but no vote is taken), and then the screening com- mittee puts through two names, in order of preference. These go to the regional ANC, then the provincial, then the national, for approval at all levels. If the first candidate is found wanting, the second comes forward. Finally, there is a list conference, which has to ensure that there is a racial, gender and Alliance balance in the names put forward.

All of this is designed to draw in, but not give control to, Alliance partners; to manage the potential conflicts; and to try and find candidates who are both popular and meet ANC standards. In fact, key members of the screening committee are able to tell me before the very first meeting who the winners are going to be, as this has been settled in an extensive set of behind-the-scenes deals. They make no bones about the fact that they have to go through the performance for the sake of appearances, but that it will not affect the result.

The public meeting to introduce the ANC's four short-listed candidates for Ward 96/113 in January 2011 is a raucous, rambunctious display of participatory democracy at work; four hours of robust exchanges about priorities, needs and personalities. It is scheduled for 5 pm on a Tuesday in a church hall, and I am surprised to find people there at that time, singing and chanting, because I have seen no posters or banners announcing the meeting and there is little in the way of local media to do the task. It is all done through word-of-mouth messages in the political structures, I am told, and boisterous street-work with a megaphone on the day of the meeting. The meeting gets under way at about 6 pm when the room is packed with about 600 people, young and old, displaying a mosaic of T-shirts from every Alliance organisation or event of the past few years, and eager to sing, shout, chant, cheer or boo.

At the front, the ward Screening Committee, which has vetted the candidates, sits quietly and earnestly at a table with an ANC banner draped over it. The chair, a young activist deployed from the ANC regional office, has a tough task ahead of him. He tells the audience that they had interviewed the candidates until midnight the previous night, and then discussed them till 4 am – so none of them had much sleep. The room is hot, crowded and noisy. The crowd is here for an evening of rowdy fun, but the chair is quick to point to those who cross the line and threaten them with eviction. Many songs are sung, most of them old struggle themes, but the one that draws everyone to their feet and is repeated most often is '*Umshini wami* – Bring me my machine gun', the controversial signature song of President Zuma.

The meeting starts with a prayer for divine guidance and a pastor's appeal for love and harmony, and the chair describes to the audience how this event fits into the ANC's new plan to involve the public in the candidate selection process. He introduces the four candidates, and it is immediately clear from the crowd response that this is a battle between the two men – the sitting councillor, Isaac Maele, diminutive, dapper and quietly confident, who is the only person in the room wearing a suit and a dress shirt, the benefits of office clear in his clothes and his bearing; and notably more casual in a man-of-the-people red T-shirt and baseball cap, Abraham Mabuke, a tall and imposing figure who speaks with strong authority. The two women, Evelyn Nkomo and Paulinah Molekoa, get no more than polite clapping from the crowd. Each candidate is given 15 minutes to answer four questions: What have you done for the community? What will you do for the community? How will you strengthen the work of the ward council? What skills will you bring to the council?

Each of them outlines a history of involvement in the local political structures, with Mabuke being able to make a show of being the only one with a university degree (in Environmental Management from University of Venda). For each one, an involvement in some way with the Community Policing Forum is central, and two candidates claim responsibility for an Absa recruitment scheme which provided call centre jobs for a number of Diepsloot people. The audience gets a chance to question them, and about 50 people are selected from the hundreds of raised hands to come forward. Many people want to make statements or demands rather than put questions, but the issues they raise are constant, ignoring the chair's pleas for people not to repeat them. When is there going to be more housing? Why is there not more land available? Why are more locals not employed in development projects? What can we do about crime? Why are taverns open all night? There is reluctance to pay for poor services. There are demands for sports fields and permanent church structures (to replace the tents many churches are using) and cultural venues. The candidates cannot address all of these issues, so the branch chair Chris Vondo intervenes to assure people that they are taking note and all the issues raised will get their attention. The evening ends at nine with a call for people to accept the outcome of the selection process and turn out to vote.

Afterwards, the branch executive is proud of being the first in Gauteng to hold such a meeting, and the display of what Mabuke called robust engagement. Their pre-chosen candidate has done well and is going to get the nod. The question will be how they contain the fall-out from Councillor Maele, who stands to lose all the benefits of office he has enjoyed and who clearly has strong pockets of support.

Two days later, I bump into Maele and he is dismissive of his rival in a way that tells a great deal about the politics of the place. Firstly, Mabuke is not a home-owner, but a backyard shack-renter. 'How can you talk to people about paying rates and services, when you don't even do it yourself directly?' he says. It is a straightforward class attack which would exclude most Diepsloot people from standing for election because they rent shacks. Secondly – and this is his trump card – Mabuke has signed every protest letter, petition and set of demands in recent years, including calling for the resignation of the mayor. 'He was always toyi-toying against the council, and now he wants to be councillor. How can that be?' Maele asks me.

It is an interesting line of attack. I understand that Mabuke is getting the nod precisely because he did these things, and the ANC wants their SACP/Sanco critics inside their tent. They want the toyi-toyers inside the official structures, so that they stop the toyi-toying.

When I speak to Mabuke, he is adamant that he only took part in legitimate, non-violent protests.

Since the protests of 2009, there has been something of a truce between the Alliance partners, with each side thinking they are winning over the other. The ANC leadership is trying to draw the Sanco/SACP leadership into participation in the process and structures of state power; the Sanco/SACP leadership is trying to get those structures to work for them, sometimes for their personal gain and sometimes for their 'community' – depending on who you speak to. They are forced together briefly for the local government elections of 2011, as they need to work together at least for the candidate selection process, and the key people are building alliances wherever they can. There is overlap in positions and membership, which obscures and confuses the divisions. But as soon as candidates are selected, those who have lost the battle turn bitter and the knives are out again. The ANC controls the process, so their chosen candidate wins out, and there will be a spate of objections, accusations and lobbying to try and change the decision. Councillor Maele is vocal and bitter about losing; Councillor Ndlazi was not even nominated again; others will feel slighted. Once the election is over, the question is whether the Alliance partners will feel they can get what they want through the new councillors or whether they will go back to mobilising their constituencies to express themselves in the only ways they can between elections: marching, protesting, opposing, demanding ...

Diepsloot feels like it is in the balance. The ANC leadership is counselling patience and understanding as service delivery is happening and more is coming, particularly housing. If they can pull it off, the power base of their rivals will fall away. If they can't, or it is too slow, then their rivals – currently taking a wait-and-see attitude – will turn back to the toyi-toyi. A great deal hangs on the planned new houses of Diepsloot East – the mating ground of The Frog – how long it takes to build the houses and the extent to which they can be used to ease the pressures in the Reception Area – the hunting ground of the Alliance partners.

Letsoalo's name comes up often as the powerhouse of the shack areas. I get him on the phone. 'I am very busy,' he tells me brusquely. 'I have a business waiting. I can't just leave it and talk to you. You must pay for my time.'

I can't pay for an interview, I tell him. But he is clear: 'I cannot talk unless you put money on the table.'

His tone is aggressive and unpleasant. This is not a man who cares too much about how he is seen from outside the shack area he controls.

Later, when I tell another Sanco leader about Letsoalo, he shakes his head: 'He told you he would not talk without money on the table? You must believe what he told you. You must believe him. He is the one who said it.' In other words, Letsoalo won't do much of anything without money on the table.

CHAPTER SIX

'If it is a blood-case, then we call the police'

We walk in single file, nobody speaking, hopping from time to time over the sewage overflow along the pathways, trying to keep our feet out of the foul, grey water. The only sound is the crunch of 20 pairs of boots on dust road and the distant music and Friday night chatter coming from a tavern. It is a dark night and the dull orange glow cast by high-mast street lighting does no more than outline the rough edges of the shacks. There is the occasional flicker of a candle or paraffin light from within one.

We are winding our way through a route so full of twists and turns that I quickly lose any sense of direction and have to just trail those leading the column who know their way through this labyrinth. Sometimes the space between homes is so tight, we have to turn sideways to get through, careful not to snag our clothing on the sharp bits of metal jutting out. The road is rough and rocky; it is easy to stumble, and the pools of murky water reflect the orange light. It is icy cold and to walk fast is the only way to keep warm.

At the front of our column are a policeman and one of the community policing commanders; another policeman is driving around the periphery in a vehicle, and will meet us when we emerge at the other end. When those in the front of our march

99

come to a street, they stop, raise an arm to signal the rest of us and peer carefully around the corner, trying to see who is there before they let themselves be seen. If they spot someone, they converge quickly on them, and the person generally puts their hands into the air, in the classic sign of submission. They are frisked. Some chat and even thank those who are patrolling the streets and searching everyone still out after midnight. One drunk man raises a stick and lashes out, but is quickly overcome by the number of patrollers – and then has to do some fast talking to avoid getting a *klap*. The stick is taken off him and he is told to get off the streets. If someone is drinking beer, the bottle is emptied on to the street and thrown down, and the person is told firmly to get themselves straight home. Three young men are stopped and as they raise their hands, we hear the clunk of metal hitting the rocky ground. Torches are shone and four knives are found lying on the ground. The four are bundled off into the nearby police van, quite roughly. 'They will drive them around for a bit, take them to the police station, and then probably release them in the morning,' I am told.

We come to a tavern packed with revellers sitting or standing in circles, each clutching a bottle of beer, while a few cluster around a fire on the road. The dull thud of percussive music played too loudly through cheap speakers bangs its rhythm into the otherwise quiet night. Those in the tavern eye us tensely, but we walk on. 'There are too few of us to go in and search them tonight. It would be asking for trouble,' the patrol commander tells me.

We stop at a shack to check if there is anyone in it. It belongs, I am told, to a gangster wanted for the recent shooting of one of the patrol members, and it is regularly checked to see if the occupant, who fled after the incident, has come back. No, the shack is locked from the outside, and we move off again in our single-file march through the huts, our boots crunching on stones and dirt. When we come across shacks with light and chatter coming from inside, a few patrollers stick their heads in and check it out. Polite but firm, with clear authority. Those inside must account for themselves. A man who has stepped outside his shack for a smoke and a cellphone chat holds his hands in the air, his cellphone glowing in the dark, while a patroller reaches over his yard fence and pats him down. He exchanges pleasantries with the group, clearly satisfied to see them out on the streets. There is no question of warrants, or cause to search, or reason to suspect a crime. When things get heated, the policeman does not get directly involved, keeping a distance. The patrollers can sort out things that he cannot. Their rules are more flexible than his, their authority of a different kind.

In the distance, we catch sight of the reflective clothing worn by 20 of our colleagues who have split off into another search-and-frisk party and will meet us on the other side of the settlement. Every now and then we see the lights of the police car that is working with us flashing in between the huts, driving around the edge of the area. But for much of the time the vehicle is driven with the lights off, slowly ploughing its way along the rough roads, looking to surprise any gangs on the streets.

Each patrol group is a mix of men and women, young and old, volunteers who are out on the streets fighting crime every weekend night, one policeman and one or two reservists. The volunteers wear variations on a loose uniform given to them by the provincial Department of Community Safety: blue jeans, black boots, caps, orange and blue windbreakers emblazoned with the Gauteng provincial logo, 'Diepsloot Community Safety Patrols' and the slogan 'Take Charge. Crime stops with me'. They carry only torches. The policemen who work with them carry their weapons. One or two of the patrollers have no uniform, as they are newcomers on probation and have not been formally inducted or trained. They still have to prove their seriousness and trustworthiness.

When we get to the end of the settlement, about a dozen of

the group pile into the police van – about eight crammed in the back and five squeezed into the front of the twin-cab – and are driven to another section, to begin another route. The rest of us wait in the shadows for the van to come back and pick us up. There is a strange, tense quiet as we peer through the murky night. This is serious work. Only about a month ago, a CPF leader was called out late at night to deal with some trouble, walked into an ambush and was found beheaded – yes, beheaded – the next morning. The patrollers who tell me this are clearly still angry about it, still nursing revenge, still on edge.

When the van returns, we pack ourselves into it. In the vehicle's lights, rats scurry across the road, large ones, perhaps one every 20 metres, and I realise they have been around us all along, silent and invisible in the dark.

It is a night with long periods of waiting, then quick marches through the houses, and the occasional flurry of noise and activity as someone is confronted. We are on patrol for about four hours, walking at least 10 kilometres. It is a relatively quiet night, with not many people on the streets, but it picks up after midnight when tavern-drinkers make their way home. The only major incident in Diepsloot that night is a man shot in the buttocks after leaving a tavern, but it happens on the other side of the settlement and we only learn of it on the police vehicle radio. The man is not seriously injured. At about 2.30 am, the police van drives around dropping the patrollers at their homes. Some will be getting up to go to work in just a few hours.

These patrols, every weekend night and some weekday evenings, have been going on since 2006, after an intervention by the then MEC for Community Safety, Firoz Cachalia. My guide for the night, the Community Policing Forum (CPF) chair, John Makola, speaks of him with fondness: 'He is a gentleman. Always a gentleman,' he says. 'He gave us these uniforms. But we do not have enough vehicles and we don't have proper communications,' and this makes the work very difficult.

The problem is apparent, as we wait for the one police van to go backwards and forwards, overloaded with patrollers. Also, the two groups working that night often lose each other, and have to use private cellphones to re-group from time to time. 'The only people earning anything tonight are the policeman and you,' John says to me. 'Everyone else is voluntary. They came home from work, and then came here. They will get home at 3 or 3.30 am, and then some will go to work on Saturday. And then they will come back tomorrow night.' There is no doubting their dedication, or their discipline.

Makola is a religious man, an ardent member of the indigenous, independent Zion Christian Church. If he does not answer his cellphone, the message tells you he is talking to his God and will get to you next. The CPF is 'a calling', he says. 'I can't tell you how many people I have buried, I can't tell you some of the things I have seen on these patrols. But I just have to do it.'

He came to Diepsloot in 1998 to stay with his brother, and now works for a contractor doing projects for Joburg Water. The CPF, he tells me, is the link between police and community, stepping into the gap because the police station is so far away and police response time is a problem. The CPF does citizen arrests. 'If someone comes and reports a crime, I cannot wait for the police. We arrest the man and then wait for the police to come.' They are trying, he says, to stop people getting emotional and taking the law into their own hands. 'I am not saying it is right, just that it does happen. We are trying to make it not happen. But when police are slow to respond, then people get frustrated and emotional, then they take the law into their own hands.' The CPF are not always well received by people, he says. 'Sometimes when they see us coming, stones fly.'

It is clear the relationship with police is interdependent. The CPF need the police for the stamp of legitimacy and authority; in turn they provide police with the numbers they need to operate in this area, and they can do things police cannot, such as sort out a quick problem with an element of restrained street justice. If the two police cars in Diepsloot operated on their own, they would not be able to venture into the side-streets at night, confronting gangs of criminals. Nor could they just stop and search.

'They cannot work here without us,' Makola tells me. The arrangement they have is a temporary one to bolster police numbers and to bring this community structure into a semi-official position. It is a first step to drawing them in while the police presence is limited. When the new police station is built, you can expect it to absorb much of the CPF's role.

Before we go on patrol at about 9 pm, there is a parade in the grounds of the Metro Police. Lined up in three rows, the patrollers are briefed by police and take instructions from their commanders. Police fill them in on a gang arrested that week in Diepsloot, tied to a string of robberies and shootings, saying they are still looking for a couple of members who had fled, and will check those shacks during the night. They are still on the track of those who killed the patrol member, and will not give up until they have found the culprits. The CPF commanders give a talk about how it is not enough to patrol, and volunteers are not coming to the CPF offices during the day to help with people's problems and complaints. And then police and commanders get into a huddle to decide where they will patrol that night. They cannot do the whole area, so will target different extensions each night. Everyone signs a register, and we split into two groups, one policeman with one group and one driving the van, and set out into the night, the vehicle chugging slowly behind.

It is no ordinary shack, the CPF office. It stands on the edge of the main road, apart and alone. Inside it has a desk and some chairs and benches, set out like a class or courtroom. An ageing desktop computer stands to one side, though I see no sign of electricity. 'This is where we deal with the community's problems,' Sam Seale tells me. 'If you came here on Sunday, you would have seen a queue of people, and we are here all day until we have dealt with every problem. Maybe a woman comes and says her husband is beating her, then we go and fetch him and here we have a hearing. We listen to both sides.' This explains the informal court-like set up.

'If it is a blood case,' he says, 'then we call the police. Otherwise we sort it out with them.'

Sam has previously made clear to me the multiple hats he wears: a leader of the CPF, secretary of the SACP branch, executive member of [the] Sanco branch and a member of the ANC.

Sam came to this area in 1998 from Tzaneen. 'Like everyone, I came to Joburg looking for a job,' he said. He is currently unemployed, though his wife and son are working and bringing in family income, while he seems to spend his time on voluntary community and political work.

He wants to talk first about crime, wearing his CPF hat. 'Crime is a big challenge,' he says. 'We have a problem of murder, we have robbery, house-robbery is escalating. The police station is 16 kilometres away, so police take their time to get here, which is why the community take the law into their own hands.'

Sam shows me a metal hoop cemented into the floor of the shack. 'If we catch someone, we tie him to this and then we wait for the police. The CPF is operating effectively, catching criminals, and handing them to the police.' They are, he implies, saving the criminals from a worse fate: 'If the community catch him, they want to beat and even kill him. Just last week Tuesday, they chased a guy after a robbery, and the other community came from that side and they caught him by the stream. They killed him.'

The CPF does what the police can't do. 'We are a bridge to the police. If the CPF is not here, there is no police here. The CPF understands this community and the community also understands the role of the CPF. When they have a problem, they turn to the CPF, not the police. But then we hand many cases over to the police.'

They have a social worker on call. 'Our big concern is the minor girls, who get raped. So then we call the social workers and they see the child, then we fetch the suspect, tie him up here and call the police.'

Will it change when the new police station is opened? 'We are going to have our offices in there. Our job will be to monitor the police, to see if are they doing their job properly, or are they taking money.'

Sam denies strongly any suggestion that they take protection money. 'We can't stop someone who is happy with our work and wants to make a donation. We can take it, but we never ask for it.'

The CPF and its evolution mark three phases in the life of Diepsloot. It was started by the community in the early years when there was no formal authority in this area, and the only way to deal with crime was for a community to organise and do it themselves. People took charge of their situation and of their lives, creating a set of rules and practices where otherwise there would have been none. It was a time when the police had no presence at all. Diepsloot was not on their map, and even if it was, they had very little capacity and legitimacy to penetrate the problem Reception Area, which then became a haven for fugitives. The nearest police station was a long way off – 16 kilometres, in fact, at Erasmia.

The CPF was closely tied to the capacity of Sanco to exert its authority, sometimes benignly, sometimes less so. In such situations, the line between self-defence and a protection racket is a thin one, often crossed. Where to draw the line between community service, community leadership and community exploitation is not always clear.

More recently, the authorities have established some presence and struck up a bargain with the CPF, taking it into a second phase. The police and the CPF work together; they assist each other; they recognise their mutual reliance. Crime is cited repeatedly by all parties as the number one issue, and the incapacity of the police to deal with it is not disputed, even by the police.

The satellite station, which for about two years was a rather sad, run-down, vulnerable-looking caravan perched on stilts in the grounds of the Metro Police precinct, was replaced in December 2010 when they cleared a patch of land on the edge of the Reception Area, put a green metal fence around it, threw down some cement and gravel, plus a new caravan for a charge office, and added five prefabricated rooms. Four patrol cars with 'Diepsloot' newly emblazoned on their sides to show that patrols were no longer sent from Erasmia, a set of flagpoles with the national and police flags, and a blue light on a pole by the entrance completed the picture. It is a simple holding operation, neat and clean, until the new station is built, but it does bring to the area and make present a small contingent of police. It means people can come and lay a complaint or a charge within Diepsloot, and not have to go the long and costly distance to Erasmia to do so.

Still, the police are outmanned and outgunned and there are night-time no-go areas for them; not surprising when one considers the narrow and windy streets in the shack areas. Indeed, the difficulties of police vehicles getting into these areas was cited as a barrier to their attempt to control the xenophobic violence of 2009. Until they have the resources to do their work and until they are able to have a presence in the Reception Area, the police need the CPF to get in and to assert a level of control and authority. In turn, the CPF needs the police to give it a stamp of official legitimacy and legality. They could go to war over control over the area, but they have chosen to recognise each other and accept the different kinds of legitimacy they each bring to the relationship.

But there is a set of rules. The police have to work with the CPF, thus strengthening their legitimacy, and the CPF have to abide by some police rules. This is all symbolised in the uniforms, the police station parade, the official register and the joint patrol.

The third phase is yet to come, when the police open their big police station and set out to absorb the CPF into their official structures, giving it offices, bringing it under the state's wing and hoping it becomes like all other community policing liaison structures in areas where the state's domain is clear and the CPF is there to serve them. The reservists will probably become full-fledged police, the community courts and CPF offices will be dismantled or converted, and the police will do their own patrols. This, of course, can only happen if the Reception Area is de-densified, and the streets opened up to official vehicles. The battles to clear the streets and gain access have been at the centre of recent conflicts, and can be expected to lead to a showdown, as the state attempts to bring its authority and power to bear. It will need to work with the CPF to achieve this.

When MmaPula caught her husband in bed with Mary, what did she do? It was not the first time this had happened. Previously, she had talked to the woman about leaving her husband alone and had been surprised to find them at it again. What does a woman do?

MmaPula took it to her street committee. Six executive members met in the house of the chair of that committee, Wilfred Makahaname, one evening in October. MmaPula presented her case, saying she would like this matter to be dealt with once and for all by the leaders of her street committee.

There was a problem: both women were members of the street committee, as was the one witness, the complainant's friend, and they were concerned that this would lead to unfairness. It might also 'cause complications' in the committee: if they found for the suspect, the other two members might be angry and abandon the structure. The case presented the kind of conflicts of interest you might expect to find in a very local dispute resolution system which was also a political structure. After an hour of discussion, the committee decided to escalate the case to a higher level, and decided to ask the Community Policing Forum to handle the case. The 'suspect' and the 'complainant' were called in to be informed of the decision, and both accepted it.

It was later reported back that the CPF had successfully dealt with and resolved the matter. Talking afterwards, committee members said they needed to group street committees into block committees where they would send cases to be settled, as they feared that some CPF members were corrupt. The ANC had undertaken to form such block committees, but it had not happened.

Street committees have a chequered history in Diepsloot. They were originally Sanco structures, a way of mobilising grassroots support which had been important during the 1980s uprising against apartheid in places like Alexandra. They were also enforcement agencies, ensuring compliance with boycotts and other mass actions. In situations of conflict and often lawlessness, such informal political structures were often corrupted to become more like protection rackets. In Diepsloot, stories of how they helped the CPF anti-crime structures were mixed with allegations of corruption and deterioration into kangaroo courts.

They were falling into disuse when the ANC's landmark Polokwane Conference of 2007, concerned about the tenuous relationship between political leadership and voters in troubled areas, instructed their branches to build street committees with the ambitious aim of relaunching them in every street covered by their branches. Diepsloot's Havana City branch, Ward 96, as ANC branch of the year, was not going to neglect such a task, but was caught up in the 2009 election campaign, when branch work had come to a halt. It picked up the issue again after the election and focused on those areas where people 'were vulnerable to being influenced to protest against the ANC', as a party official put it. The political purpose was explicit: 'to penetrate and counter the plans to destabilise the ANC by the SACP and Sanco in the ward'.

They started in Extension 12 and thereafter Extensions 6 and 7 were the subject of an 'intensified campaign that saw all members of the ANC in the ward going out to launch and explain the purpose of street committees', according to ANC branch documents. They found a reluctance, 'as many still remembered how street committees were managed and run in the 1980s ... and believed the era of mob justice was returning to haunt them'. But the ANC was sensitive to this, I was told by a branch leader. 'Issues of integrity were of the utmost importance to the ANC and this was explained carefully. The public behaviour of any person standing for election [to a street committee] was scrutinised to make sure they had no skeletons in their cupboard.'

A document laid out a wide set of purposes for these committees: to facilitate service delivery; to resolve personal disputes, 'but not to entertain boyfriend and girlfriend issues'; to monitor shack erection, but not to give or withhold authorisation, rather to take these matters to the housing authorities; to assist the CPF in fighting crime; to encourage responsible behaviour by residents by becoming role models; and finally, and perhaps most importantly, to discourage any rebellion against the ANC.

In short, it was an ANC push to seize control of street structures and displace those of their rival Alliance partners.

They reported success, saying that within a month they had street committees set up in every extension. The ANC undertook to return in a month or two to group the street committees into block committees. They told the committee to select a house on each street as their meeting place, usually the house of the chair, or to use outdoor space where that was available. They also undertook to offer training, and scheduled a community hall meeting every Monday at 5 pm for street committees to report on their work. These meetings took place for a while, then came to a halt. The block committees had not been formed by the end of 2010.

The ANC itself is aware that 'some of these committees have collapsed and others degenerated into kangaroo courts where people are beaten up and made to pay fines'. Where this was identified, 'the structure was replaced with a new one'.

Street committees were complaining of the lack of a support structure and were being pulled apart by political conflict. 'Where the ANC chairperson and the councillor do not see eye to eye, the street committees are forced to support one or the other.' Some complained that they often invited a councillor to their meeting, and he promised to come, but never did.

MaSetjaba leads me on a winding path through the shacks, on a precarious plank over a stream of sewage clogged with plastic and other waste, to a small piece of open land alongside the water, and points to a black patch in the dust. 'You can see there has been a fire there.'

At about 3 am on Saturday, two days earlier, a crowd had set fire to a man named Boy Maluleki at this spot. I had met MaSetjaba courtesy of a local Methodist priest, who said she would tell me a lot about Diepsloot. She told me about this incident of mob justice that happened just near her place at the weekend and I asked her to take me to the scene.

'I heard the noise, but I was too scared to come out of my place,' MaSetjaba says, showing me where she lives, about 30 metres away. 'The next morning someone called me to come and see.'

A few metres away a group of men sit in a circle on boxes and crates, talking. 'Did you see what happened here?' I ask. They shake their heads and the circle closes again. Children scurry around, playing in the sand, oblivious to the black ashes in the soil. Music booms from a nearby tavern with a few drinkers slouching around outside, watching us. It is clear that nobody will say they saw the incident; nobody will want to admit they know who was there when it happened. This is not a helpful line of questioning. People here are moving on.

In the shack which Boy Maluleki had allegedly attacked, I find Costa and his sister, both of whom are reluctant to give me fuller names. She is bathing a small child in a bucket of water. One wall of the shack is lined with books, including a set of *World Book* encyclopedias and a *Good Cooking* book. 'It was between two and three in the morning,' he tells me. 'He just kicked the door down. It was fixed with a lot of nails, but he just kicked it in and threw a bottle at me. And he threatened to shoot me.

'I said "Just take what you want." He told me to keep my head under the blanket so I could not see him. He walked in and was going past my bed to my sister's room. That's when I grabbed him and jumped on top of him. My sister shouted and whistled and everyone came running.'

Many of the women of Diepsloot carry whistles. Blow it and people come running to help.

'I was on top of the guy on the couch and they took him off and pulled him outside,' Costa said. 'By the time I pulled on my pants and shoes and came outside, the man was burning.'

How many people came to help? 'Whew, I don't know. The whole community came.'

Was the attacker drunk? 'He was a bit drunk, but he had all his power. I fought with him and he was strong.'

Police came the middle of the next morning, took away what was left of the body and told Costa, his sister and mother to report to the satellite police station. 'I accepted that because it is the law,' Costa says. The three reported there, and, Costa says, one of the policemen began shouting and swearing at him, calling him a 'murderer'. 'I got angry and started to beat him. It was only the other policeman who stopped us.'

They were taken to the Erasmia station, questioned about who did the burning, made to give affidavits, and locked up. There were kept through Saturday and Sunday night, and taken to court to face charges on Monday, but the prosecutor said there was no case against them and they were released.

'But they lost my cellphone,' he says. 'When they locked me up, they gave me a receipt for my two cellphones and R5 I had in my pocket. But they only returned one cellphone. They told me to come back Tuesday and they will sort it out.

'Now the man's family are threatening us. They say they will go fetch his brothers in Soweto and they will come and burn our shack.'

That's one version of the story. Boy Maluleki's family have a different perspective, and it is this one that appears in the *Daily Sun* on Monday morning:

'He was very drunk when he arrived home and knocked on the shack door asking to be let in.

'When no one answered, he forced the door open.

'But it was the wrong door!

'And the family inside, thinking he had come to attack them, screamed loudly for help. Neighbours responded and beat the intruder to death and then set him on fire!'

His elder brother, Packs Baloyi, told *Daily Sun*: 'My brother did not deserve to die like a thief. He was not armed and if he was lost they should have helped him, instead of calling the community who killed him. We want justice to take its course ...'

Police said three people had 'handed themselves over'.

The *Daily Sun* is not a paper to compromise a good headline by acknowledging more than one version of the story. Truth is hard to establish, and a sense of justice a hard thing to hold on to in Diepsloot, where the grey areas between right and wrong are not as clear as they are in places where there is the rule of law, proper lighting and doors which can be securely locked. With no police around, with brutal crime levels, people are vulnerable in rickety shacks. Strengthened by a strong sense of community, they have developed a system to assist each other: whistle, shout, and people will come running to help you. They will use numbers to overcome even armed groups of thugs. With little faith in the justice system, they sort it out then and there, decisively and brutally, with the help of a bit of paraffin and the hysteria of crowds. It is hard to be righteous about due process when people know that it is beyond their grasp, and hard to condemn vigilante justice when it is the only kind of justice that is available. There is an indistinct line between self-defence and vigilantism, and that line is littered with the bodies of the innocent as well as the guilty.

In this case, as in all such cases, police will open a file and never get anywhere with it. They will never know who killed Maluleki and we will never know where either he or his killers fell in that continuum between innocence and guilt. But the matter is fast forgotten in Diepsloot and it is only a few hours before the burnt black spot gets trampled into the dust, and children are playing there.

This kind of vigilante justice happens in regular spates. The *Daily Sun* reports it with delight and even relish, amidst a flurry of apostrophes and capital letters, and the safety of anonymity. Almost always, the vigilante action was done by 'the community' and they quote positive reactions from 'residents'.

On 8 January 2009, their headline screams: 'Justice is ours! Angry crowd tries to block cops'. The front page is dominated by a picture of a grinning crowd manhandling a bloodied man and the story reads: 'Leave People's Justice free to do its work.

That was the cry from angry people who cornered four suspected thieves.

'[They] blocked surrounding streets to keep the cops at a distance. While the police broke down the barricades, the township crime fighters gave the trapped suspects the beating of their lives.' The four armed men had robbed a Pakistani storekeeper, and when three were confronted by a crowd, they fired warning shots, to no avail. They were showered with stones until they surrendered. It took police 30 minutes to break through the barriers of rubbish bins and rocks.

On 12 January 2009, the paper tells of a crowd going on a thug-hunt: 'People went after the rest of the criminals involved in the [previously reported] robbery ... Each time the crowd found an alleged member of the gang, they beat him until he blew the whistle on fellow criminals. By morning, they had four battered men. They had also recovered stolen goods.' The *Daily Sun* was outraged that police charged one and released three for lack of evidence. 'The community said they were sick of the poor service they got from the police. "Nothing comes from the cases, so we will do the job ourselves," one resident said.'

A few weeks later brought the story of a man killed for stealing chicken feet. 'Roasted ... the thief who ran away with runaways!' was the headline.

'Everyone loves runaways – tasty chicken feet cooked to perfection. This 24-year-old guy was a great lover of the treats,' the *Daily Sun* said. The man helped himself to some from his neighbour's pot, got caught and 'angry people in Diepsloot – the town that takes no prisoners – grabbed the guy and beat him to death! Then they set his body on fire!

'It happened only a few hundred metres from the local police station. And it's outraged the area's new top cop who says there will be no more People's Justice under his nose.

'But local residents said: "We only call the cops to collect the bodies!"'

And in May 2009, the paper reported that a man was beaten because someone recognised the skirt his wife was wearing: 'A man paid his cousin R25 for a skirt for his wife, but now he bitterly regrets doing it ... The skirt was stolen.' When the woman from whom it was stolen saw it on another woman, she was furious, and angry residents beat up the man. He 'only just escaped death' when cops rescued him, and his wife returned the skirt. 'I would strongly advise everyone to stay away from stolen goods,' he said.

The stories of 3 and 4 November tell of the impunity of criminals, and how ordinary people confronted this: a gang had attacked tavern drinkers, leaving one person dead. 'But they were so arrogant they went back to the same place'. They were spotted and angry residents 'made them pay ... they beat them up, stoned them and set them alight as the men pleaded for their lives.' When police arrived, one was dead and two others taken to hospital.

On 23 February 2010, a woman is reported calling for help and then saving her rapist from her neighbours. 'She saved the thug that tried to rape her!' was the headline. She screamed when a knife-wielding man broke into her house and tried to rape her, and the neighbours came and caught him. 'They gave him a heavy beating and were preparing to finish him off! But he was saved ... by the very woman he had attacked!'

A few weeks later, a group of women caught someone trying to rob a domestic worker of her salary and cellphone, stripped him naked and made him walk 'a march of shame'. The front page of the paper was dominated by a picture of gleeful women wielding large sticks over the pantless man.

New methods emerge all the time. In July 2010, the paper reported that a hacksaw used by thugs to break into a shop was used to cut off their earlobes.

And there is the occasion when it emerges that the wrong person was killed, as reported on 30 July 2010. 'They thought it was Peoples' Justice. They thought what they were doing was good. But it soon went horribly, horribly bad.' An angry crowd stoned and hacked to death a man who had been identified by a woman as a robber. But two weeks later, cops found out it was a case of mistaken identity.

Figures for the number of such incidents are not available. Police bury their Diepsloot figures in a much larger regional picture. The *Daily Sun* said in November 2009 that 19 alleged criminals had been killed by residents in the 11 months of that year, and several others injured. 'Several residents face murder charges for taking the law into their own hands.' I could find no example of such a case going to court. I could also find little discussion of this issue and its frequency in areas such as Diepsloot. It was as if – like xenophobic violence pre-2008 – it barely existed in most of the media.

The new police station looms above one of the main entrances to Diepsloot, an imposing three storeys high in an area of low-roofed shacks. It is still under construction but is going to be one of the largest police stations I know of, and its arrival is hailed by all as an important moment. It will be a coming of age for Diepsloot when the station opens its doors, rolls out its vehicles and personnel into the streets of Diepsloot, dusts off its charge office desk and brings the case files and investigations from distant Erasmia to the heart of this settlement.

The symbolism of the station screams out. Standing like an apartheid-era structure of control at the main entrance to the township, it represents the introduction of the rule of law, of order where there is chaos, of authority where it is disputed. Law and order are the tools of incumbent ANC leadership, those who want process and patience and control, and the enemy of those who farm shacks, who run mob justice, who lead the toyi-toyi and who want to control where police may or may not go. But these are not the only signs of lawlessness: there is also massive theft of electricity through illegal connections, in addition to unregulated trading and all the other more regular signs that Diepsloot represents a vast gap in the rule of law.

Most people will undoubtedly welcome police who catch murderers and robbers and make it possible to walk around at night without fear. But will they all welcome police who might also stop illegal cabling, which is keeping many houses going during winter? Will they impose licensing and proper business practices on the traders? Will they contain the taverns, who they serve and when they do it? It does not help that people are massively sceptical of the police and their commitment to law and order, and believe most officers are on the take.

The police are going to have difficult ground to traverse to assert their authority here. And it will be crucial to the struggle for political control of the area. The station is rising above the township as an icon of state hegemony. At the moment, though, unfinished and unused, it stands instead as a monument to the budgeting and bureaucratic limits to the state's capacity to bring its presence to bear in this township of violence.

During October 2010, the South African Police Service and the Department of Public Works, who oversee such projects, came to Diepsloot to explain why work on the station had ground to a halt. The way this was handled says a great deal about the relationship between the state and the people of Diepsloot. First, they met the ANC leadership. They explained that the project is under judicial management 'due to the mismanagement of finances and other labour-related matters'. It seems that an employee had misappropriated R20-million from the contractor and R4-million that Public Works had paid over for the job to be finished had been frozen, so that the contractor could not pay his staff and sub-contractors. Everything had ground to a halt.

Now they wanted to form a joint monitoring team to oversee the outcome of the judicial management and the outstanding issues of the police station. It was resolved with the ANC to form such a joint team, made up of a community liaison officer (there's employment here!), the two councillors, representatives of SAPS head office and the Erasmia Police Station, the Department of Public Works, two representatives of the ANC, and one each from the ANC Youth League, Sanco, the SACP and the Young Communist League.

A few days later, there was a broader meeting, at the youth centre. This time an SAPS representative talked about work opportunities. SAPS has a contract with a cleaning company that cleans all of the properties, and they will need one cleaner and one security guard for every 1 000 square metres. SAPS will endeavour to use local labour. A further meeting will be held at which SAPS human resources will be present and community members will be put on the database so that they are accommodated when this work starts. The joint committee is announced.

So that is how things work: the state consults with the ANC, then it has a wider meeting of all the Alliance partners, the main concern of which is to apportion out the contract and employment opportunities which arise.

The Commissioner of Police, the meeting is told, has ordered that the station must be ready by March. Clearly this is a date set with the coming local government election in mind, though it is an entirely unlikely deadline. When I come back three months later, the site is still dormant.

CHAPTER SEVEN

'Foreigners can have no more than two shops'

Seven people sitting in a circle on cold-drink crates in a bright red converted shipping container – not what one might expect for the meeting of a local business chamber. Yet I have stumbled into what is perhaps one of the most important meetings of all business people that day in July 2010, shortly after the football World Cup, when there were widespread fears of an outbreak of xenophobic violence. Diepsloot traders have come together to thrash out a way of dealing with the tensions between them, which they fear will fuel violence.

'I am one of those who suffer because of the Pakistanis,' an elderly woman explains to me. 'They have opened two shops next to me and now there is no more business.'

At the meeting are six traders, one of whom is the leader of the Foreign Traders' Forum, and a local Sanco representative, all of them members of the planned new Diepsloot Chamber of Business (Dicob). They are meeting in the shop of the Dicob chair, a telephone rental business in a shipping container painted Cell-C red, with car batteries dotted around the floor connected with car starter-cables and their outsized crocodile clips to an array of cellphones. The shop has been closed for the morning to allow for this meeting. I am late, so the circle is expanded and another crate produced, brushed off and a piece of newspaper put on it for me to join them.

They have thrashed out an agreement which will be reduced, they say, to an affidavit to be lodged at the Erasmia Police Station. Foreigners, they have agreed, may not open any new shops and those who have more than two have to close the others. In return, the shops that are there already will be accepted. Everyone is happy – the locals have limited the competition which has been killing their businesses, and the local foreigners – those already entrenched in Diepsloot – have got 'protection'. Both parties will keep out new intruders in the delicate balance of local trade and commerce. 'They [new foreigners] will have to go to town. There, no one can stop you opening up a business,' they tell me. The Sanco representative is there to put a political stamp on it, and because Sanco is like the Commissioner of Oaths, no agreement will hold water without its stamp. The paperwork at the police station will be shown to any newcomers so that they can see the agreed ground rules.

In the all-South African spirit of negotiating an unlikely peace agreement, they have collectively redefined 'foreigners'. It no longer means simply those who come from other countries. Now the locals and the foreigners already inside the ring are agreeing to keep out new foreigners, those not yet in the ring. It is the insiders – both local and foreign – keeping out the outsiders, the potential competition. It is a cartel, but one unlikely to fall foul of the country's strict competition law. It is also another example of an informal, on-the-ground attempt to deal with the absence of normal rules and regulations. In Diepsloot, people just open shops without having to register any companies, or take account of any by-laws or zoning rules, or have any papers or documentation for themselves. The state legal structure is absent, so they have created their own, by mutual compact. Even if reduced to an affidavit as proposed, this agreement would hold no legal ground, but with the local business and political organisations behind it, and the just-below-the-surface threat of a repetition of the horrific xenophobic violence of 2008, it might hold sway in Diepsloot for a while at least.

The chair of the Foreign Traders Forum, a Pakistani named Shahid Butt but known as Mandoza (the name of a well-known musician, oddly, and nobody, not even him, could tell me why), had been among the very first to be attacked during the 2009 violence. He had arrived in Diepsloot a decade earlier, brought to this country by his 'brothers', and opened up a small shop in Extension 1. He lived in Erasmia, 15 minutes' drive away, where presumably the police station held sway and he was relatively safe. But that terrible day in May 2009, he had fled his shop and lost everything to the looting and burning. It was weeks before he ventured back, and then for a long time he had loaded his stock into his car every night and taken it home, so as to reduce the risk of losing it again.

Things have normalised over time, but now that tensions are rising again and there is new talk of xenophobic violence, he is taking a new approach, teaming up with his business rivals – and, by implication, his potential attackers – to keep out others who might disrupt the equilibrium they are trying to establish between them. (He had stopped ordering new stock a couple of weeks before this meeting, just to be safe, and had again been loading up his car on weekends with his most valuable stock and taking it home, out of Diepsloot.) He is promising, as an unwritten element of the agreement, to get the other foreign traders, mostly Pakistanis and Somalis, to give more to the community, such as blankets, shoes and food for crèches. His business chamber will call a public meeting and have a handover of such gifts. 'I will say to people, look, I am helping you. If you have a problem, you must come to our office and complain. But we must not have this xenophobia.'

'If all the traders talk like him, there will not be a problem,' the chair of the Local Traders' Forum and owner of the cellphone shop, Colin Shai, tells me. Francinah, from Sanco, says: 'We are trying our level best not to have xenophobia here. Most of those who do it are criminals, they are just hiding behind xenophobia. We tell them that if we catch you, you are in trouble. They know what we will do to them.'

They discuss where they will open an office to deal with these issues. Some Somalis have just opened up their fourth or fifth shop, and they will have to close them down in terms of the agreement. 'If we take one over [for an office], then we will be helping them,' Mandoza says.

The violence began on 14 May 2008 in the Reception Area and lasted five days, spreading to Extensions 2 and 4. It was a case of contagion: 'comrades', youths from the informal areas, had seen on television the attacks on foreigners in Alexandra township and a meeting had been called to discuss it. At least some intended that the meeting should prevent such violence in their area, but that was not the view that prevailed. Shortly afterwards, the youths started apprehending people to check their papers. They attacked both foreign nationals and local minority groups, such as Shangaans and Pedis, sometimes in error – mistaking them for foreigners – and sometimes deliberately, telling them to 'go back to Pietersburg'. They showed no discrimination in targeting men, women and children, and destroyed, looted and burnt down their businesses and houses.

By all accounts, police made an effort to intercede, but struggled partly because the violence broke out sporadically in different places and partly because they had difficulty penetrating the Reception Area, made worse by road barricades, congestion and a shortage of manpower. Mostly, outnumbered, they kept to the fringes of the area.

As best as I can ascertain, nobody died in Diepsloot. A number fled during those few days, but they returned shortly afterwards. Across the country, 62 people died, some of them burnt alive in front of the world's media, and some 35 000 people were displaced. It was the worst and most sustained civil unrest the country had seen since the arrival of democracy. It was a moment when we South Africans looked into the darkness of our collective soul and realised how fragile and uncertain this democracy was, how spots of deprivation like Diepsloot were staining the whole tapestry.

I am struck in my time in Diepsloot by how much is being done to discourage xenophobia. In my first week of research, in the days after the World Cup, I walk into a local day-long workshop which has drawn about 30 key people to discuss the problem and how to prevent it. Organised by the city's Migration Desk – upgraded since the 2009 violence and now with a dedicated Diepsloot officer – it follows a similar workshop in Soweto, with another due to be held in Alex. I also attend a follow-up meeting in the local council offices to plan the launch of a Diepsloot Front Against Xenophobia. Its aim is 'to mobilise to fight against Xenophobia' and its mission, scribbled on a whiteboard, shows how the issue is seen as integral to the future of the place. They will 'work together to build a community that promotes democracy, integration, diversity and development in order to build a spirit of ubuntu'. They proclaim 'zero tolerance' not just of the mistreatment of foreigners, but of 'all forms of discrimination, social exclusion and xenophobia'. Everywhere I look I see posters quoting President Jacob Zuma on the need to be tolerant of foreigners, and every meeting I attend of any sort includes a talk on this subject. A business chamber meeting ends with a current version of an old struggle form of call-and-reply: '*Phansi* xenophobia, *phansi*,' the speaker chants, fist in the air. (Down with xenophobia, down.) The crowd chorus, '*Phansi, phansi.*'

A few things are consistently said on this issue by the scores of people – not just leaders, but all sorts of citizens – I speak to in Diepsloot. The first is to discriminate between foreigners who have papers and therefore some official recognition of their right to be here, and those who do not, and are responsible, it is repeatedly said, for much of the crime. This does not quite gel with the evidence from 2009, when the comrades demanded to see people's papers to identify foreigners, not to differentiate which ones were there legitimately. There has been a change of sentiment, at least verbally, in that the leadership has shifted the focus on to illegal, undocumented foreigners, who are being told they have to go to the Department of Home Affairs and sort out their status. 'We help them to do that,' local leadership told me.

ANC ward chair Rogers says: 'We say the law must take its course. We must get an understanding of the status of foreigners: what happened when they arrived here. We have some who have asylum, other who are here for political reasons, others for work-related issues. It is a pity that people only look at the bad part of it. There are some elements involved in crime activities, but there are also professionals, teachers and intellectuals from those countries who contribute to our economic growth in this country.'

And then there are the street traders, whose frustration is palpable. They cannot compete with the foreign traders, they say, because so many new shops are being opened, and because the foreigners are able to undercut their prices. The foreign traders have the capital and resources to buy in bulk. Asking around, I discover that some of the foreigners band together to buy as a unit and use their collective weight to force down prices. The locals are consistently frustrated at their inability to match this, which they usually blame on their lack of capital and the unhelpful attitude of the banks in providing the credit their businesses need.

Of course, foreigners offering cheaper goods are popular among the shoppers. It is the local traders who cannot compete, and whose anger is making everyone nervous.

But another factor emerges. Dicob leader Lucas Loate tells me he has come to believe that many of the foreign traders are just fronts for a larger businessperson who has recruited and brought them in to set up these shops. Behind these foreigners are South Africans who are funding the large stocks and the building of shops. 'How else do they arrive and move so quickly to have these big, well-stocked places,' he says. 'I am investigating. We will have to stop this fronting.'

In the political rivalry of the area, each side blames the other for stoking up xenophobia. The shack farmers, I am told by ANC leaders, stir up feelings when they need a new source of income. 'You see, there are people who make money from it. When they are short of money, they chase foreigners away and then they can charge them again when they come back.' There is little doubt that the toxic local political rivalries feed into the xenophobia.

The most common thing said, though, is that the violence is essentially criminal. Young thugs taking the opportunity to do some looting, no more than a form of collective, opportunistic redistribution of wealth. President Thabo Mbeki, speaking at a memorial event a month after the violence, said it was not the result of xenophobia, but rather of 'naked criminal activity'. He did not talk, though, of the context. It was those with little or nothing using the opportunity to seize something from the closest, most accessible and most vulnerable source.

The Pakistanis and Somalis who tend to run the bigger shops are the target. The smaller street traders seem to be better integrated into the area and express little fear of being victimised as foreigners. Njabulo Sibanda is a 25-year-old who came in 2007 from Harare and now lives in Extension 5. 'I buy for the same prices as other traders and sell at the normal prices.' He has not experienced xenophobia. 'We all live together nicely,' he says.

Amkela Sibanda, 30, arrived in 2009 and rents a room in Extension 1. He started trading three months previously, selling the standard fare of oranges, small packets of chips and sweets. 'There were no jobs in Zimbabwe and no opportunities. I came to Diepsloot specifically because I have relatives that live here, so it was easier for me to find a place to stay.' He lives from hand to mouth and does not even calculate how much he makes in a week. 'Sometimes I make just enough to live and buy food for that day. Sometimes you find you don't even have money to go home that day.' He has not experienced xenophobia and again does not understand the suggestion that foreigners sell things cheaper: 'It's all the same because you can go all over Diepsloot and you'll find that everyone sells at more or less the same price so it doesn't really make a difference.'

Sipho Ndlovu, a Zimbabwean who came to Diepsloot in 2007, lives in Extension 5 but has been trading for only about three months in clothes, socks, fabric and hats. 'I came here looking for a job, but I still have not found one, that's why you find me selling here. I finished my matric and there were no job opportunities in Zimbabwe.' He lives in an area where there are only foreigners, so does not interact much with the locals. 'Where I live and stay, it is just us foreigners.'

Sanki Ndlovu is 36, came from Bulawayo in 1998 and has been trading in Diepsloot since then in the usual small items: chips, popcorn, sweets, cigarettes, matches and lollipops. 'I came here looking for a better life, but I'm still struggling. I came to Diepsloot because the rent here is cheaper for foreigners.' On xenophobia, she has heard stories of people being attacked, and is aware that 'there are some people who want us here and some who don't', but, 'I have good relations with my neighbours; I have never experienced anything myself'.

Eric Msebele came from Maputo in 2009 and now lives in Extension 5. He has been trading for six months: 'I can't find work in Mozambique. There is no work. I came here because there is a few people I know here.' He only makes about R150 per week. 'We have no money, and we don't make enough here and money is scarce,' he says. He has not experienced any xeno-phobia, saying, 'We have no problems here, we live in harmony.'

The estimates I get of the number of foreigners in Diepsloot cover an impossible range – from 18 per cent of the whole area to 60 per cent of Reception Area. It sums up the difficulty I have in finding any statistics that help make sense of Diepsloot. The city's 2008 Poverty Study says 18 per cent of its sample of Diepsloot residents were of non-South African origin, but this figure is dismissed by most of those involved in the area. Indeed, it is likely that illegals shy away from surveyors clutching clip-boards and asking touchy questions. But this also reflects the uncertainty and rumour in the country as a whole, where one can hear from respectable sources (such as an economic consult-ing firm) that there are as many as nine million foreigners in the country illegally, a plainly ludicrous number. Such figures 'gener-ate a kind of popular panic combined with official resignation and passivity,' one commentator concluded. 'It was this toxic reaction that probably contributed to the attacks on foreigners.'

The official census figure for foreigners is 2,6 per cent of the national population, or 1,26-million people. Statistics SA's 2007 Community Survey, which simply asked people where they were from (and is therefore almost certainly a serious under-counting) found 300 000 foreigners in Joburg. An attempt at a systematic estimate comes from the Centre for Development and Enterprise (CDE), which surveys 1 000 homes, interviewing 300 immigrants as well as business organisations, police, local government, immigration and welfare officials. They conclude that there were 550 000 foreigners in Joburg (in 2008), includ-ing both legal and undocumented; around 14 per cent of the population. Forty-one per cent of these, they say, lived in in-formal housing areas like Diepsloot, indicating clearly that the percentages in those areas would be significantly higher than the average. Perhaps most importantly, they say that only 20 per cent of the foreigners were unemployed, almost half the average among South Africans, and a very high 41 per cent were self-employed, including 12 per cent who employed an average of four other people, of whom half were South Africans. Seventy-five per cent said they would go home to retire, though 'in reality, far fewer actually do so'.

They talk of discrimination within the discrimination: some foreigners are more foreign than others. People from Botswana, Lesotho and Namibia, Westerners and Indians are 'highly approved'; Chinese, Zimbabweans and Mozambicans 'approved'; Malawians and Pakistanis approved with qualifications; Nigerians, Somalis and people from non-English-speaking African countries (except Mozambique) 'do not gain approval'.

CDE puts this down to those who 'dress, look and speak differently'.

More important than the numbers, though, is to understand the role foreigners play, or are seen to play, in Diepsloot. This falls into three categories.

Firstly, foreigners are blamed for a good deal of the crime. The main source of information in this regard, the ubiquitous *Daily Sun*, delights in giving the nationalities of criminals whenever they are not local. And, it has to be said, this is often the case. The *Daily Sun* famously responded to the xenophobic violence by saying that it sympathised with those who were fed up with foreigners. 'Many of us live in fear of foreign gangsters and conmen. Much terror has been caused by gangs of armed Zimbabweans, Mozambicans and others.' The paper made a small concession: 'Not every foreigner is a gangster, of course – but too many are.' It is a sentiment I hear all the time, sometimes combined with the view that the criminal ranks include former Zimbabwean guerrillas, heavily armed.

Secondly, the foreigners are seen to be uncompetitive traders, using their combined strength, skills and access to capital to steal the livelihoods of local traders. There are too many small traders in Diepsloot for the amount of available cash there, and the foreigners are the ones seen to be arriving and setting up often a string of shops selling at lower prices.

Thirdly, a number are seen to occupy the most sought-after asset in the area: houses. Many South Africans who are granted RDP houses do not have jobs or sufficient income to sustain the costs of the house. Many turn the house into income by sub-letting parts of the house or the yard. Thus most RDP houses in Diepsloot are surrounded by up to 10 shacks crowding the yard, generally at about R250–300 rental each. A third option is to sell the house, and a significant number of sales are to foreigners, who will pay a premium as it may be their only way to acquire property and – as the CDE figures show – enjoy relative prosperity. Sales have to be cash, as the sale is illegal and the banks will not back it, and prices are low. What others see is that a foreigner has acquired a house in an underhand way and they do not have one themselves – and may have been waiting for some years for one. Foreigners have bought their way to the front of a long queue.

Throw in an opportunistic criminal element – enough unem-ployed youth hanging around at any time to take advantage of uncertain situations to help themselves to some goods and supplies. And, underneath it, think of a foundation of political rivalry with intense competition over resources and control, and this gives you a number of political structures and influ-ences ready to use tensions and incidents as weapons of politi-cal influence. The result is a cauldron of conflict, a volatile and precarious broth, prone to outbursts of conflict and violence which can take the form of xenophobic violence, or service delivery protests, or mob justice – or some unpredictable mix of these.

There is an overlap between the xenophobic violence and the so-called service delivery protests, largely because each outbreak of protest has been accompanied by attacks on foreign-owned shops. Also, mob justice is often about what the state should do, and doesn't, and this feeds into a notion that issues with foreigners have to be sorted out in the same way because the authorities are not dealing with them.

There have been three spates of protest in the last two years in Diepsloot. Each of them calls into question whether the term 'service delivery protests' is not just a convenient journalists' shorthand, and often a misleading one. The first outbreak, on 5 July 2009, was sparked by a rumour that the occupants of up to 2 000 shacks were to be moved to Brits, north of Pretoria. In fact, 320 shacks were to be moved to the Adelaide Tambo section of Diepsloot to make way for new and badly needed sewerage pipes. The current pipes cannot cope with the population and replacing them is a critical step in the rehabilitation of the settlement. The affected shacks were to be moved to another area and the promise was that these families would get RDP houses when they were ready.

Councillor Ndlazi appears to have briefed all parties on this about a week before, but at a meeting on 5 July the Brits rumour was spread and this led to a protest which turned violent. It is not clear if the rumour was spread maliciously, but the ANC leadership blames Sanco leaders for this, suspicious that they did it to solidify their own position and support in the Reception Area. Being moved in this way is a touchy subject, as only a few of the people who had been brought 'temporarily' to Diepsloot a decade earlier to allow for development in Alex had got the proper services and housing they were promised. Government policy is to move people only once – so to do it again, and repeat the promise that it was only temporary, was always likely to draw disbelief and resistance.

'Diepsloot in flames', 'Diepsloot on fire', 'Diepsloot on knife edge', 'Diepsloot mob go on the rampage' were some of the headlines of the next day, as shabby in their grammar as in their accuracy, promiscuous with both clichés and truth. About 300 people were involved and they had stoned cars and blocked the R511 road that runs alongside the settlement. That was when police opened fire with rubber bullets, chased fleeing youngsters into the shacks and arrested about 14 of them. In most reports, it is clear that the problem was a false rumour, but it is still put down to unhappiness over service delivery or 'RDP hopes [being] dashed'. Much is made of Councillor Ndlazi arriving at the scene in an armoured car.

Some see it as part of a wave of such protests across the country, a copycat action – and there appears to be validity to this, as each of the Diepsloot outbursts came as part of a countrywide spate of such outbursts. This same week saw protests in Mpumalanga, Cape Town and Rustenburg. But there is no doubt the core issue in Diepsloot, the spark that set it off, was the threat of being moved. 'It was because of wrong information given to people about removals,' a city representative says. Chris Vondo, ANC branch chair, blames 'a complete distortion of information'.

The *Sunday Times* quoted a participant: '"We are going nowhere," yelled 34-year-old Selby Mukovhanama as he waved a panga in defiance of a government plan to dismantle the Diepsloot, Johannesburg, shack settlement.' Note how the problem has become the destruction of the whole settlement. Much as the authorities and the people of nearby Dainfern might dream of this, it was never on the agenda. 'They want to dump us in another slum, without clean water, electricity and sanitation. We are not going anywhere. If we do move, it must be to decent RDP houses,' the *Sunday Times* quoted. This was more likely an accurate depiction of what was happening – those who were being moved seeing it as a chance to get the maximum out of it.

Some used the cover of the protest to target shops. 'They broke into an Indian-owned shop and stole everything. The owner sells clothes and DVDs,' the *Sowetan* reported. 'Criminals took advantage and looted shops,' was the way *Pretoria News* put it. Resident Phineas Mudau, who rents shops to Pakistanis for R750 a month, was quoted saying: 'Thieves saw this as an opportunity to loot and destroy shops belonging to Pakistanis.'

Another common claim was that it only got violent when police opened fire with rubber bullets. 'Looting and vandalism would not have happened if the police had not shot at the peaceful march,' Joe Masemola of Sanco told the *Mail & Guardian*.

A repeated claim was that Sanco was using the incident for its own political purposes. One of the more thoughtful reports came from the *Saturday Star*: 'This is about the politics of the stomach, where individuals seek attention and advance their ambition to public office by embarking on all sorts of dirty campaigns against those elected by the community.' It quoted Councillor Ndlazi saying he was not surprised by allegations that Sanco was involved: 'Sanco has been a problem, not only in Diepsloot but in all informal settlements recently.'

A week later, the protests broke out again for a day. And in October, they took a different form, starting with a march led by Sanco and the Communist Party against the corruption of councillors. Police declared the march illegal, and used rubber bullets to disperse it. Nineteen were injured, including one policeman, and a photographer's motorbike was burnt. Communist Party Youth League leaders were adamant they had permission for the march and that it only turned ugly when police disrupted it.

An incident in January 2011 says much about how easily trouble can be sparked in this volatile area, and how it comes to be seen and handled in the outside world. A gang of about 17 terrorised a shack section of Diepsloot on a Friday night, shooting dead a man who resisted them and wounding the woman with him. Residents say they tried to call the police, but the satellite station commander was not available and one of the two patrol cars was out of order. The crowd took the matter into their own hands, caught two alleged culprits, beat them to a pulp and then locked them in a shack and set it alight. Police arrested seven residents who they accused of being involved in the lynching – and this infuriated residents, who gathered angrily and had to be dispersed.

It is not difficult to see the reason for anger and frustration with the authorities. Not there when they are needed, the police arrive the next day and make the easy arrests. They target those who take the law into their own hands before they go for the thugs. Yet it is hard to blame the police, since they don't have the resources or numbers to tackle the gangs at night.

The provincial MEC for Safety and Security comes the next day to hold a public meeting to address the issue. She has been briefed, she says. She does not want to see 'criminals being arrested and released back into the communities'. She wants to see a 'Friends of the Court' system put in place to enable communities to make it clear when someone should not be released back to the same place. There is a boundary problem, she says, in that Diepsloot still falls under city of Pretoria jurisdiction and this needs to change so they can confront these issues. But, she emphasises, 'taking the law into your own hands is wrong and criminal ... you will be jailed.'

People have lots of questions: When is the police station going to be finished? Will there also be courts in the area? Who benefits when you are told not to take the law into your own hands? How can people trust police who are taking bribes? But the MEC has to rush back to Freedom Park where she is dealing with a threat of xenophobia. 'I am going to leave my officials here to take your questions and make sure that all challenges will be noted and fixed. I must go to the Premier to report these matters.'

And she's off.

This incident was a spontaneous crowd response to crime, but when I interview Sanco and Communist Party leaders, they have no compunction in telling me they were behind most of the protests of the past few years. They were excluded from the decision-making and kept in the dark over developments, they say, and they had to force the ANC leadership – which had grown away from their constituency – to take note of what people were saying.

'Now they are listening to us,' a Sanco leader says to me.

CHAPTER EIGHT

'There shall be houses, security and comfort for all'

Sitting in a central Johannesburg steel and glass office tower, a long way from Diepsloot, Shingai Mpinyuni takes me through the Gauteng province's plans to develop the settlement. He is a director in the housing department, an upper-middle-level figure in the bureaucratic web. I find him in a small, plain office with simple furniture that carries the feeling of government drab, somewhat at odds with the shiny, corporate feel of the building. It is a downtown corporate headquarters abandoned in the northward flight of business, and rescued by provincial administrators. Mpinyuni talks animatedly about Diepsloot, with a focus and passion undiluted by the fact that he has to deal with at least six other difficult and similar settlements spread across the province, all competing for attention and funds.

Mpinyuni has a sense of drama as he takes me through the narrative. He shows me detailed plans and colourful maps that lay out extensive research, thinking and planning at provincial, city, regional and local levels. He runs through the history of what has been achieved so far in Diepsloot – some houses, some electricity, some roads, some sewerage, some government buildings, half a police station – and what still needs to be done: most importantly, tackling the demand for housing and unpacking the dense and difficult Reception Area. He explains to me who has what authority over development, dispersed between national government, the province and the city, and he sets out the role of the Treasury, parastatals and the private sector. It is a bag of jigsaw pieces that have to be put together to make things happen.

He explains the overall policy as dictated by central government, the choices which have to be made in his provincial office about where to spend the money they are allocated, and how the city with more arms than a Hindu god is the final implementor. City agencies will oversee the actual work, executed by private contractors, subject to provincial approval. He talks to me about whether or not the state provides only land, or land and services, or land and services and housing, or housing with services, or separate plots or dense accommodation, or some combination of these options; of the need to deal with those who only want to rent rather than own, the undocumented and child-led households, how one fits in shops, and clinics, and schools, and parks and sports facilities. He talks to me about the arduous process of getting approvals at each stage of the way. He outlines complex negotiations to buy land and sign deals with private developers, all along having to keep the banks on-side so that they will play their part in giving bonds for the bigger middle-class houses. He talks about the complexities of people accessing the housing subsidy scheme at the core of government funding and dealing with those who are not eligible for subsidy. He has even taken on board the recommendations for dealing with The Frog. The breeding area is left intact and the plan is to start building in the north and move gradually southward.

As he nears the climax of his complex and engaging tale, he draws himself up for effect. 'Within about six months,' he says, 'I will have approval for our plan for the next stage of development in Diepsloot.' He looks up and takes a deep breath. I am made to wait a moment for the denouement. 'Then I will file it away over there,' he says, waving his hand towards a shelf behind him, 'where I already have six files of such plans waiting to be implemented.'

I look over, and lined up at one end of a wooden government-issue shelf is a set of files not unlike the one he has on the table in front of us. They are in a neat row – static, silent and accusatory.

The issue, from Mpinyuni's perspective, is funding. He can draw up all the plans he wishes – in fact to meet his job requirements and tick off his key performance indices he has to churn them out – but the financial numbers say it all: 'We are underfunded to the order of about a tenth of what we need,' he says.

The plan he has shown me is for Diepsloot East, the next phase which is intended to deliver about 7 000 houses – about a quarter of the current need. His provincial housing allocation is roughly R4-billion a year, 25 per cent of the national total, of which R1-billion goes directly to local government for specific projects. That leaves him R3-billion to deal with four regions, which get R700-million each, and each region has four sub-regions, which can expect about R125-million each. If all Region A's money just went to Diepsloot, and he ignored competing needs in the region, it would take seven years of budget to complete the plan, which meets only a quarter of the settlement's needs. 'And it will cost more if we wanted to do it quickly,' he says. 'Politicians always come in late, and then want it done quickly.'

The plan he is working on is not in this year's budget, or next year's, or in the three-year medium-term budget which drives government spending. 'So I will get to a place in about six months where I have all the plans and permissions, and I will file the project over there, with all the others that are ready with plans and permissions, because there is nothing further I can do. When the politicians ask what is happening with Diepsloot, I will take the file down, show them what needs to be done, and tell them that as soon as there is budget, we will start to build. The next day.

'Hopefully, the politicians will make a plan.'

To understand the official plans for Diepsloot, it is necessary to go to a number of national, provincial, city, parastatal and private sector offices dotted around the city centre and as far afield as Midrand and Pretoria. There is the national Treasury which allocates funding, the national Human Settlements Department and Ministry which sets policies, the provincial housing office which decides how the money is going to be spent and approves the plans, and then the city agencies responsible for implementation. Joburg's city administration is broken into a number of different, independent agencies, run as not-for-profit companies – Joburg Water, Joburg Power, Pikitup (which deals with trash), the Joburg Property Company and the Joburg Development Agency.

There are a multitude of different levels of political oversight to learn about: the national Department of Human Settlements, the Ministry and the parliamentary committee; the provincial premier, the MEC for Local Government and Housing, his committee of the provincial council and the council itself; then the city Mayor, his mayoral committee, his council committee, his Director of Housing, and the bureaucracy that answers to him, including directors of each city region. That is not to mention the Ward Councillors, their Ward Committees, and the political parties they report to, as well as their allies.

Then there is a pile of elaborate and complex, colour-coded policies and plans to work through: the national housing policy, as set out in the 2004 'Breaking New Ground' document, the National Housing Code, the National Spatial Development Perspective, the Minister's key policy and budget speeches and presentations; the Premier's State of the Province speech and annual budget which outlines annual priorities, and those of the relevant MECs, the provincial Growth and Development Strategy; the city's Growth and Development Strategy, its Integrated Development Plan, its Local Economic Development Strategy, the Spatial Development Framework, the Regional Spatial Development Framework, the Five-Year Integrated Development plan, the Five-Year Housing Plan, the Urban Development Plans, Development Plan for Diepsloot, Central Sub-Region Precinct Plan, the Regional Urban Management Plan, the Diepsloot Development Framework, the frameworks for each individual project and all the illustrations, research documents and appendices which fill these out and turn them into impressively long and detailed but barely readable tomes. Throw in also the Development Bank's Policy on Sustainable Development, its Diepsloot Urban Renewal Project Business Plan, and its Diepsloot Project Implementation Plan and a bunch of supporting research they have generated. Never mind the work of academics and researchers who analyse, comment on and debate this material.

An arcane new language of urban renewal – with phrases such as 'nodal developments', 'daylight sewers' and 'activity streets' – has to be digested, with a rich tagliatelle of acronyms like UDP, RSDF, PPPs and COEs.

But little of this will assist you in understanding the essential questions: what is holding things up and how long are things going to take, why does there appear to be so much activity and planning, and so little to show for it? For that you need those closely involved to explain their challenges and frustrations, and for every pile of documents you plough through you find individuals who are keen, dedicated, skilled and smart – who offer their own perspective on the hold-up to progress. The best way to get through this morass is to listen to those who grapple their way through it daily. Each person in each different department, though, has a different perspective, a different finger to point, their own complex explanation.

Paul Arnott is a senior development manager in the Joburg Development Agency, a traffic engineer imported by the city management from England back in 1975. He rose to assistant director in city transportation, then moved to work for the city itself to build taxi ranks. When the JDA was started in 2001, he was transferred into it, making him, he says with some pride, 'a founder member'. The JDA does big projects for the city – what they call 'area-based economic development initiatives' – mostly dealing with public spaces but working alongside those in separate entities who deal with specific services, like housing, water and power.

'It is incredibly rewarding work because you can see you are making a difference to people,' Arnott says. 'And I am damn sure we [in JDA] can do it better than anyone else in the city. We deliver huge projects on tight deadlines and budgets – and we usually make it. We are very proud of it.'

JDA's offices are in the Old Bus Factory, a warehouse structure in Newtown, the downtown Joburg cultural precinct which has been one of the major JDA projects. The office is urban regeneration trendy, signalling a working culture different from traditional municipal structures. The art on the walls is very local, very contemporary and quite spunky. Indeed, JDA are known for their effectiveness and boldness in doing things like using public art as part of their inner-city rejuvenation. The place has a young, energetic, corporate feel rather than the dullness of a city bureaucracy.

For the first few years of the new government, Arnott tells me, JDA's focus was on Soweto, the Mayor's home town and his political priority, but the city had largely achieved its vision there and now the focus was moving to areas like Diepsloot. Two years ago, the city's Department of Urban Planning requested funds from National Treasury's Neighbourhood Development Programme for Diepsloot, with JDA to oversee the implementation. In 2007, Treasury approved R8-million for technical assistance and R92-million for or capital (infrastructure) expenditure.

JDA, according to Arnott, was asked to do an Urban Development Framework (UDF) for what they call Diepsloot's district node – a particular chunk of the settlement that would need housing, public transport facilities and places for trading and other commercial activities. In fact, they decided to draw up a framework for Diepsloot as a whole, in order to generate options for what projects to undertake. 'We wanted some new ideas, some options for interventions, which we could take to public consultations.'

They settled on three projects. While the province's focus is the grand housing project of Diepsloot East, the city's focus is on developing public areas with a particular view to improving life and facilitating commerce and investment. They set their sights on:

- The Government Precinct, the stretch of road where most of the official buildings stand, such as the police station, the fire and ambulance station and skills development centre, as I have seen on my visits. This involves the main road into Diepsloot West, upgrading the taxi rank, fixing the market area along the road, stormwater management and sidewalk paving, street lighting, street furniture and landscaping.
- 'Activity Street', the central artery to be developed into an economic and business node. In fact, it is called Ndimatsheloni Street, and it is a lively thoroughfare, linking the Reception Area to the more formal areas and lined with retail and service trading and industry as well as dense housing right on the edge of the road. To make this the hub of local activity, as they envisage, they will need to make pedestrian walkways, provide informal trading facilities, upgrade the road itself, manage the storm water, fix the open spaces and put in street lighting.
- The district node. This involves taking one chunk of the settlement and putting in high-density residences, public trans-

port facilities and facilities for retail and informal trade and other commercial activities.

They put the work out for tender and it was won by a consortium of engineers, quantity surveyors and experts in community liaison, including 26'10 South Architects.

As you might expect of a practice called 26'10 South Architects (based on their geographic coordinates), they work out of a converted shopfront amid the devastated Vrededorp area on the edge of central Joburg. The Indian residents of Vrededorp were forcibly moved out at the height of apartheid, most of the buildings were razed and the area has never recovered. It is still a brutal scar on the edge of the city centre. 26'10 rents one of the graceful old buildings which survived; restored and renovated, it now stands among the ruins, a living symbol of what they do in it: develop ideas and designs for urban regeneration. The office foyer includes a display of their innovative work. The key people are a youngish man with the unlikely name of Thorsten Deckler and his wife Anne Graupner, and they have some bold ideas about what to do with areas such as Diepsloot.

While they were working on the JDA brief, a tender came up to deal with the whole Reception Area. Thorsten attended the briefing and asked some pointed questions. It turned out that key people had been to Mumbai to see a development plan for the notorious Dharavi settlement. The plan was based on the notion that the lack of adequate housing was just a symptom of broader socio-economic challenges and a holistic approach was needed. The Mumbai authorities called it Hikes: Health, Income, Knowledge, Environment and Socio-cultural development all had to be addressed simultaneously. Even more innovative was that it was to be privately funded: the private sector was to be invited to tender to take over the whole area, invest in and develop it and profit from the way they used the land and whatever they put on it. The City officials were so impressed they recommended that a similar approach be tried out in two of Joburg's most difficult areas: Diepsloot and Kliptown.

Think out of the box, they told Thorsten excitedly. If we gave you all the land, what would you do with it? They threw out a challenge: think about the whole development, from top to bottom, every element. And think how to make it self-funding.

That may sound like the kind of brief one would want from a forward-thinking city, but it was extremely difficult, if not impossible. Thorsten's experience in dealing with Activity Street illustrates why. The JDA had to do something with Activity Street, even if it meant just starting with fixing the road, which was in appalling condition. That sounds simple. But it had been done before, and the road had deteriorated quickly because of the poor drainage around it and the sewage running through it. Without proper stormwater drains and adequate sewerage, the summer rains would wash the road away again. But informal structures – mostly commercial – had been built right up to the edge of the road, so you could not deal with the road and give it a proper shoulder without moving the traders and other businesses, and some houses. You would disrupt the very businesses you wanted to promote and develop. You would have to go through complicated negotiations, overcome resistance and mistrust and then, hopefully, move them without causing a riot. This is a difficult, uncertain and potentially explosive process. Besides, the JDA don't do housing – that is a separate department. There were some prototypes drawn up and JDA were keen to try the project, but it could not be done without the Housing Department, and they were not ready for this.

'We have to go to community participation meetings and tell people what we want to do with the street,' Thorsten says. 'But they say they want houses. Where are the houses, they ask? And we have to say we don't do houses, we are doing this for the JDA and the JDA does not do houses.'

The project that did get a quick go-ahead was the Government Precinct. Money came through for this and had to be spent within a few months. They had a good contractor who moved fast and a solid road was built, the walkways were paved, impressive street furniture installed, and good lighting. It is the one part of Diepsloot the city can be proud of. It is a stretch of about 200 metres of Diepsloot's 66 kilometres of road.

The projects for Activity Street and the other nodes have not got beyond the drawing boards.

At one consultative meeting, people said there was an urgent need for bridges over the water to make it safe for the children who had to cross it every day. A number of bridges would be needed but they settled on two for the first year, three the following year. Everyone was extremely positive: the community had indicated an unexpected priority, and the city was responding. This was the essence of consultative, participatory development, a textbook case. There were difficulties: to build the bridges, you had to move some shacks. Who was going to do that? Fortunately, places for the bridges were found which required only a shifting around of some shacks. With some talking and nudging, this was done voluntarily and building started about six months later. It included some space around the bridges for traders and pathways that would link living spaces with schools and other facilities. From the first suggestion of bridges to the completion of the first two will take close to a year.

A big part of the problem is coordination, according to Thorsten. To get these projects done, you have to bring together the JDA, the housing department, the national and provincial financers and the power, water and cleaning entities in the city. They each operate independently, have their own priorities, pressures, demands and ways of operating. During 2010 they were brought together into the Diepsloot Development Forum, and began to meet regularly for the first time to share information about what they were planning for the area.

'The system is not very integrated,' Thorsten says politely. 'There are high-level plans across departments, but there is little coordination between them. Either there is no funding, or you have to spend it quickly or lose it. And so you spend it on quick, piece-meal projects just because it has to be spent before the financial year-end, or it will be returned to the Treasury.'

It is not the developers who are slow, he says, it is not those doing the work on the ground. 'It is the political process which holds it up. You need innovative decision-making, but JDA managers are also terrified of the awkward questions they will be asked about these decisions when they are audited. Things are dampened by a by-the-book approach, so the easiest thing to do is paving and other piece-meal upgrading of public spaces. These don't address the structural issues underlying the challenges people face in places like this.'

The issues of budget allocation are difficult. Joburg Roads has a huge demand for tar roads in settlements like Diepsloot across the city. But it has a limited budget, which it divides up between them. Diepsloot gets R10-million, which allows for about 2 kilometres of road a year (given the amount of draining and related work that has to be done). At this rate, it will take 30 years to tar the roads.

The situation is worsened because there is so little maintenance being done. The tar roads are falling apart, and the untarred so uneven and rock-strewn, often with streams of sewage and stormwater running through them, that they are near impassable. The sewerage system reached its capacity about five years ago, and now it constantly overflows and runs through the street. The only time I saw Joburg Water paying any attention to it was when there was going to be an event, one that would attract outsiders into the area and perhaps some media.

The Development Bank combines the scale of big government and the flash of corporate banking. To get into its Midrand offices, you have to park outside, go into a security area, get approval and sign in, get back into your car, go through a car security check, drive through large grounds, park again, go through a front-door check and wait for your host to come and get you. Clearly, this bank supports job creation in the security industry.

I first connect with the Bank when I bump into a young engineer, Orapeleng Letsholonyane, in the streets of Diepsloot. Geo, as he is called, is committed to the settlement and its development like no one else I've met. He is a fit and strong long-distance runner, and he has brought this staying power to Diepsloot, determined to make the Development Bank's partnership with the city work. He is open and chatty, but before he'll go on the record, sends me off to see his masters at the Bank. Xolani Ndungane, the head of sustainable development, is the man I have now come to see.

Straight off, Xolani says he had wanted to pull out of Diepsloot, so frustrated was he with lack of progress. It's only Geo's determination and his MD's orders that have kept them there. He thinks Geo might be damaging his own career by sticking with a project which is making so little progress, but also backs his enthusiastic young colleague. 'We were spending a lot of money and not getting the support of the city. Geo is in there paid for by us, and we gave them substantial resources for planning. But there was too little progress.'

A few years ago, at the instigation of then Finance Minister Trevor Manuel, the Bank expanded from its work in financing development projects into actual delivery, and it became 'an implementer and integrator'. It started to hire engineers and technicians, rather than just bankers. It launched its sustainable communities arm, working out how it could tackle difficult areas and work with stakeholders to put long-term integrated development in place. Diepsloot is one of the six target areas identified.

In April 2007, the Bank signed an MOU with the city which did not lack ambition or scope: they undertook to work together to 'provide appropriate housing and accommodation and associated municipal services to all the residents of Diepsloot in a way that will instil human dignity, create economic opportunities for local people, strengthen the "sense of place" and community and have a positive (or minimal negative) effect on the environment; to improve the social, economic and environmental functionality of urban space [which implies] higher densities, integrated residential areas, linkages between places of residence, recreation and work and organisations around transport modes and nodes; to introduce sustainable practices; to focus on poverty eradication and the promotion of human dignity'. To do so, they would develop a social compact with the community, review the Diepsloot Development Programme Business Plan and all existing projects, conduct an in-depth investigation of available resources, formulate a Local Economic Development Strategy and mobilise financial and human resources to accelerate implementation.

Whew! Just reading the agreement is trying; getting one's head around the scope of it is exhausting.

The worst thing the city ever did, Xolani says, was to set up the City-Owned Entities (CoEs) to separate out the departments of water, power and other services into independent structures. 'To do anything now, you need so many approvals. They behave as if they are entirely separate organisations.'

The other problem is that Diepsloot is not a formal township, as it was only established as a reception and transit area. Now they are having to get it approved as a township, and that means taking financial responsibility for it. 'At the moment, the province has responsibility, but they are not obliged to provide municipal services. The city has to be careful about taking financial responsibility because a whole lot of obligations come with that.'

The Bank can only support and assist, as the municipality

has to do the actual work. 'We pulled out of Motherwell [in the Eastern Cape] because the municipality could not do the work. In Diepsloot, the original plan was a full-scale intervention to deal with it all, but we have had to scale it down, because there isn't the political will to deal with it.'

One of the biggest problems is to get one's head around how to deal with illegal foreigners. 'It is the most accessible area for foreigners. About 40–50 per cent of the people there are illegals. That is one of the things the city does not want to deal with. But if you don't deal with that, you can't deal with housing. The minute you put houses there, you realise that many of the people are not eligible for housing.

'So we need to agree: how do we define the community? Does it include foreigners? If so, which foreigners? Legals and illegals?'

The Bank started with a Status Quo report in 2007 and put R5-million towards this – the only holistic attempt I could find by the authorities to establish the make-up and needs of Diepsloot. They estimated at the time that there were 120 000 people, and the number was growing at 20 per cent per year. The initiative included a land use study, to identify what you could put where, and a housing study to identify requirements. 'The misconception is that you need housing. You need accommodation, not housing. In December, or over Easter, the place is empty, as people go back to their homes. If you put houses there, people will sell them and move.'

'We have struggled to get a political champion for this project,' he says. 'We created a partnership with [building company] Group 5, to train the unemployed. It is the third year now, and we have struggled with trainees from Diepsloot. There was no real interest from the community, there was no one there to do it. Out of about 30 students from there, we ended up with about 12.'

Xolani has a banker's contempt for those who fix the blame

for non-achievement on a lack of budget. 'The one thing we don't have is a shortage of funding. We are short of appropriate models for development, and the skills and resources to implement. There is no overall plan. There is money allocated for Diepsloot, but how is it being used? We have all these channels for interventions, but nothing really happens.'

The Bank assisted the city in getting the R100-million Neighbourhood Development Grant from the Treasury, but about half of it had to be sent back, he says, because it was not used. 'They started squabbling and not implementing. The city will say things are happening – look at the police station, the clinics, and so on. But for me the issue is, what is the overall plan? What you need is a major intervention, not to tackle the soft issues.'

Now the Bank was starting small, with a trial sanitation project. 'We tried to start with housing for two to three years, but nothing happened. Now we have a private company which has come up with a sanitation solution. It is a closed system, and does not have to be linked to any external system, so that is interesting, and we can move faster on that.

'We approved a test with 10 toilets in the Reception Area. We want to see if this offers a solution. We have to work with the community in it, as they have to monitor and look after it. We will set up a sanitation forum, to ask how we should deal with it. This might take a year or two, and then we can look at housing.

'We have funding, we have asked Joburg Water to procure the sanitation project. We approved the funding for this almost six months ago and transferred half the money to them. Then they said this technology did not meet minimum standards. So we said send the money back to us. Then they sorted this problem out. But the money still has not been spent.'

An example of the co-ordination problem is indicated in a formal note from Joburg Water. In their R13-million upgrade of sewers and toilets, they needed to move 300 shacks that were on the waterline. 'The department concerned was not of assistance in the relocation procedure, which made it almost impossible for the contractor … There was also a misunderstanding that people relocated would be built new shacks. Political differences within the community also played a role in the delay.'

A further issue was 'vandalism on the toilet structures which put the contractor in a difficult situation of not being able to hand over complete toilet structures … and he has to replace what has been damaged.' The solution was a 'community awareness programme' and 15 facilitators were appointed to go door-to-door in the area 'to educate about the toilet system, its usage and the causes of blockages'.

Geo is not in a rush to contradict his superior, but he shakes his head sternly when I ask if it is true that there is a lack of political will in the city. He deals every day with the structures and individuals involved, and it is there that his frustration starts. 'There is political will, there is.

'The problem is internal administration politics. The city has all these internal structures which make things very complicated, unlike a small municipality where you have a few people in one building. With this city, you have to talk to the regional director, who reports to the executive director, you have to go through the whole council, with resolutions, to get things into the system … you have to go through public participation, and council committees, before you even get to the City-Owned Entities. This project has to get onto the list of priorities.'

You also have to take account of the fact that you are dealing with communities and leadership where literacy and skill levels are low. 'You can tell from the questions we get in meetings. All the councillors are young, they are not yet established. In the ward council, the oldest guy is 45. They still want to prove themselves. I am not sure if they have passed matric. We have to discuss council matters, but I am not sure if they understand the system.'

He has difficulties with conflict of interest on the ground: how can the project liaison officer also be the chair of the ANC branch, for example?

Like so many people, Geo fluctuates between saying how much has been done, and awe at how much more has to be done. 'A lot has changed in Diepsloot since 2008, and there is a lot happening now.' But on the detail, the frustration emerges. The police station is being built, and was due to be finished last year, but there has been no work on it for five months. There was another school being built, and that was 80 per cent finished. There was a push to do sports facilities – and this could be a quick fix – but there wasn't enough land to do it. 'And if you build sport facilities without houses, or use the space for houses for a stadium, then you have trouble.' The sanitation project has been held up for six months because of 'the whole compliance thing'.

Back to Thorsten Deckler to learn more about his plans. Thorsten has no difficulty thinking big and bold. He does big and bold.

The first thing you need to do in a place like Diepsloot is throw out the notion of de-densification, he says. This is a startling thought, as so many politicians have told me this is the priority, that everything depends on this. De-densification is a magic word. But you have to move away from the vision of RDP housing – the matchbox house sitting in the middle of a plot lined up in neat and spacious rows, Thorsten says. With a shortage of funds and land, and a need to make service and transport models work, you have to increase density, not decrease it. There is just no space to give all those shack-dwellers RDP housing as well as schools, parks, sports fields and other basic amenities. Forget it. It is a dream. These are the hallucino-

genic promises of politicians at election-time. These are townships put together by engineers rather than architects and town
planners, design based on the underground service lines rather
than built around people, communities, families and their complex relationships. They produce sterile areas, with few public
and community spaces. 'Low-density settlements laid out exclu-
sively around minimal service provisions and rendered lifeless
through rigid zoning by-laws are not addressing the housing
and socio-economic crisis in South Africa,' Deckler writes on
his website.

These rigid, one-size-fits-all housing schemes do not take account of the fact that there are many people who are not enti-
tled to subsidies or state-granted housing, or who do not want
to own houses (at least 25 per cent of the Diepsloot population),
and therefore have to be accommodated in some way (unless,
as in Alex, you are going to export that problem to yet another
settlement). Maybe these people do not have the documentation
to entitle them to housing, maybe they are foreigners, legal or
illegal, maybe they have houses elsewhere and are in the area
temporarily and do not want to put their resources into immov-
able assets. They also do not take account of what I have seen in
Diepsloot: that with high unemployment, many people cannot
afford their houses and will either sell or rent the house or some
of their plot, and the area will quickly re-densify.

Thorsten has a different vision, based on 'a mixed typology of
housing'. Build a mix of big, small, flat and three- or four-storey
housing, clustered housing, for purchase, for rental, with commercial and community and private space mixed in. Thorsten's
vision is busy and bustling, streets lined with four-storey walk-
up housing and commercial space at street level, perhaps with
people living above their shops. Density would increase. Houses
would be designed with space to rent, or in clusters including rental units. This would allow people to generate income
through rentals, and accommodate those who are not going to

own. If renting is going to happen, at least make it orderly and planned, and not the messy, random way you currently find in Diepsloot, which leads to formal housing quickly deteriorating into conditions not unlike the shack areas. Renting space in private houses is done all over, so why is it being discouraged in RDP houses?

Thorsten pulls out an aerial picture of the Diepsloot shack area and a schematic drawing of the distribution of shacks. When you stand in the street or walk around these shacks, they appear randomly placed, haphazard and disorderly. But from above he discerns a pattern: shacks are in small family clusters, bunches of them sharing small courtyards and fenced off as units. 'Diepsloot functions like a hotel for Joburg. You pay R1 000 to own a shack. It is very accommodating and versatile, but from outside you can't see what it actually offers.'

People have structured the space to serve their needs, he says, and it means that child-headed households, for example, get the support and assistance of their neighbours. Each housing cluster is a small support and security network, with people watching out for each other. You do have an existing housing structure, he says, it is just one that is not handed down from the state. Shops are where people need them, often within that cluster. 'They have organised their dwellings in a way that suits how they live.' This is confirmed later on when the daughter of a tavern-owner shows me how for security they have positioned family houses around the business to provide hidden storage and control access. This cannot be seen unless it is pointed out.

To break this up into dispersed RDP housing is to break up these 'units of support' and tear apart the social fabric which, in a poor area, is vital for survival. 'If you could work with the arrangements which exist, take what is happening and improve the physical foundation, that could be your plan,' he says. A sensible plan reproduces and uses these structures to make a new settlement stable and viable.

One way to do this is with *in situ* upgrading: establish people's ownership of their space, apportion land on the basis of how they have shared it between themselves, accept the spatial relationships they have negotiated for themselves, and give them security of tenure where they are. Then fix the infrastructure and amenities around that.

But government sees an informal settlement as something that must be 'eradicated', 'de-densified' and 'formalised'. What Thorsten is saying is fundamentally different to what I have heard from the politicians.

Give people tenure and it is likely that at least some of them will start to improve their own housing. At the moment, they wait for promised RDP houses, they wait for government to act, and there is little incentive to do much else. The 2006 social survey showed that only 10 per cent of those in the Reception Area said they had made improvements to their dwellings in the last five years. Yet only 5 per cent were satisfied with their living conditions.

Another way is a gradual approach: take two of the yards, relocate those families temporarily, implement a solution and move them back. Take it step by step, cluster by cluster.

'You have to recognise that there is an economy going on here. There is a landlord who is managing tenants, making profit, and so on. There are people happy to pay them for the space. But that is being outlawed, for example when you put an RDP house in the middle of a plot precisely because then it is harder to put shacks around it. Why not build a cluster of houses, around a courtyard, which is how people live and probably want to live? Or look at a house with rentable rooms?'

There is a report in the newspaper in the very week I talk to Thorsten, a stark demonstration of his point. The MEC for Human Settlements in the North West province visited a new housing settlement and made what her own spokesperson called 'a startling discovery': an RDP house rented for R700 per month by a businessman operating a tuckshop while the owner lived on a nearby farm. The angry MEC gave the businessman 14 days to remove his belongings, it was reported in *Business Day*, and said the owner would be deregistered and the house given to someone else on the waiting list. 'These houses belong to the needy,' the MEC said in her own media release. 'We will not allow people to use them for personal profit.' As the article pointed out, the MEC did not have the power to eject the tenant or confiscate the house, and had contempt for the notion that one should make profit from one's property or that one might make a rational choice as to how to get the most out of it. She was depriving two people of their livelihood and trying to impose a fake and unworkable social structure.

Indeed, the government is so set in this attitude that it was included in the ANC's annual policy statement on 8 January, 2011. 'ANC branches should assist in eradicating the problem of people who receive new houses, then rent them out and move back to informal settlements, causing government to chase moving targets. This irresponsible practice has to stop,' President Zuma said.

'There has been an overemphasis on de-densification,' Thorsten says, 'but you don't have the land for it. We could build housing typologies that can accommodate even more people in the Reception Area than there are now. We can create an enabling housing structure through flexible ground floors which allow for shops under houses, lots of rental opportunities, shared public spaces and amenities.

'There is enough land, if you know how to use it. Flexibility is required. The subsidy needs to be used differently.' And here is the next problem: the system is based on one family unit, one house, one plot, one subsidy. It is built around matchbox housing, as rigidly as the service pipes that run under the ground and ensure that the houses are all in neat rows.

When I arrive to meet the Joburg regional head of housing, Nomsa Mlotshwa, she is dealing with an overnight crisis: a fire in the KyaSands settlement which has destroyed shacks and left a few hundred people homeless. She has been at a 7 am meeting to arrange for material to help those affected to rebuild. She turns down my suggestion to reschedule, has me wait a few minutes, takes a deep breath, and we sit down in a dour Midrand office park for what is to be a long and wide-ranging discussion.

'As much as we are hoping to have all the typologies of housing,' she says, 'government is not ready for this. There is a disjuncture between policy and budget.' By this she means that there is no allowance yet for the fact that multi-storey housing would cost more, nor does the subsidy system allow for the sectional title arrangements you would need for this.

'It costs R48 969 to build a 36 square metre basic RDP house, with two bedrooms, a bathroom, a lounge and an open-plan kitchen. Lately, instead of making that structure bigger, we have decided to work on the finishing: plastered on the outside, two coats of PVA inside and sandcreting for the floor. Then there is not much more for the owner to do, except put in a ceiling.

'That is where the subsidy takes us. The need is for more high-rise and more rental units – but we are going to need to spend more money on this. If you are going to build a stack-up, say seven-floor, the foundations are more expensive.' She gives precise figures, but is in fact a bit out of date. The current subsidy for a 40 square metre RDP house is R55 706. The subsidy to acquire and put in services for a freehold site is R22 162, leaving the occupant to put in what is called the top-structure. But that does not change the problems she is pointing to.

'The system is not ready to deal with sectional title. To build one larger unit, we would need two or three subsidies, and our current system does not allow for that. And there is concern about the dependency syndrome. Government wants to build houses and step away, not be involved in managing them or worrying about rentals.'

'There are more people in Diepsloot than the land can accommodate. We have to go high-rise, but who is going to fund this?' she asks. So for now she carries on deciding whether to make matchbox houses a bit bigger or give them another coat of paint.

The focus is now on mixed-income development – allowing for not just RDP houses, but also higher-income, private sector developed and funded units. Government has introduced a special R1-billion fund to assist those in 'the gap market', who fall between the indigent who need a free house and the middle class who can get a bank bond. Mixing this housing up in areas such as the planned Diepsloot East frees up additional funds and allows for cross-subsidisation. But it means that services have to be top-level, meeting middle-class requirements, and housing has to meet the banks' standards, so that there is no insurmountable discrepancy between the houses. People are starting to buy into this idea and the private sector are warming up to it, she says. 'I don't know if it is because we have evolved, or because we have run out of options.'

But all of this takes time and considerable effort. And it will only deal with a fraction of Diepsloot's needs.

A number of people involved in the city tell me to speak to Steve Topham. He is a development consultant who came out from England to work in this country some years ago, and has been immersed in city administration and development issues for some time. He will be able to give me the big picture. We meet in a coffee bar in the old Joburg suburb of Kensington, and talk against the background of a loud argument about money in Portuguese, the lingua franca of these parts. Topham takes out large sheets of paper and makes drawings and graphs and scrawls words to illustrate his story. Like so many people I speak to, he is passionate and animated, and a mix of bewilderment and frustration comes bubbling quickly to the surface.

South Africa has built the remarkable number of about 2,5-million houses since 1994, and continues to do so at the rate of about 220 000 a year. The exact figure is disputable, depending on what and how one counts, but there is no denying the scale of it, making it what the authorities claim to be the biggest state housing delivery programme in the world outside of China. 'Housing delivery has been one of the strengths of the government,' wrote two urban planners, Melinda Silverman and Tanya Zack, in 2009. 'It is one of the state programmes benefiting the greatest number of people.' Or as the Banking Association of SA said: 'The success of South Africa's housing programme is unparalleled, and we can be proud of our achievements.'

In that same period, though, the number of informal settlements spread around our cities has gone from 300 in 1994 to 2 700 in 2010, with 1,4-million inhabitants. In 1994, the need was for 1,7-million houses, or 16 per cent of households; in 2010, the need is 2,1-million, or 17 per cent.

So the battle to house people is being lost, the promise of the Freedom Charter ('There shall be houses, security and comfort for all') receding, along with the pledge of the constitution ('Everyone has the right to have access to adequate housing'). Money is being poured in, a massive bureaucracy is dedicated to providing housing, along with a private sector industry, but the number of people needing and demanding housing is outpacing the delivery rate, impressive as it is. In the Minister's own estimation, the backlog can only be cleared at a rate of about 10 per cent a year, and the number of people who are inadequately housed is increasing daily.

After taking power in 1994, the ANC government introduced a new rhetoric for housing development, but continued to provide much the same kind of matchbox housing inherited from the apartheid technocrats: two bedrooms, one bathroom, living room and open-plan kitchen, between 30 and 40 square metres in size and sitting in the middle of a standard plot, with electricity and water, lined up in neat rows. Most townships built in this way were sterile and inefficient: there was little development other than housing, few public spaces or communal facilities, little allowance made for trade, and the low density made public transport inefficient. The politicians were promising lively suburbs and better housing, but the rush for delivery meant that old models were being used. In fact, much of the engineering work – and it was development driven by engineers looking for the most efficient way to lay pipes rather than urban planners concerned with the quality of community life – was done by the very same people who created apartheid townships. Because large tracts of land were needed for such developments, they tended to be on the peripheries of cities – and the old spatial apartheid was reinforced.

The new government took flak for the quality of housing, especially when they had to cut corners to speed up delivery – like slapping down shoddy houses without any services when they ran out of time and money and elections loomed – but there seemed little prospect of providing a higher grade of accommodation. Budget and demand just did not allow it. 'The most visible manifestation of state housing delivery is in the form of RDP houses, orderly rows of standardised, mass-produced units on the peripheries of our cities,' Silverman and Zack wrote. But there was 'a fundamental mismatch' between this modernist vision and 'the messy, postmodern reality of today's urban milieu'.

The RDP housing model assumed 'full employment, social stability, aspirations to orderliness, impermeable nation states, nuclear family arrangements, and homogeneity'. But the reality of South Africa was 'high unemployment, mobility and migrancy, intensified transnational flows, new household arrangements that are very rarely nuclear, and hybridity'. The gap between policy and reality was a chasm. Even official documents recognised this: 'Despite all the well-intended measures, the inequalities and inefficiencies of the apartheid space economy have lingered on,' it was admitted in 2004.

'Breaking new ground' was a shift in policy, produced as part of the government's Ten Years of Democracy review. Accepted by the cabinet in September 2004, it talked not of housing but of human settlements and promised 'to move towards more responsive and effective delivery'. It called for a more flexible, more community-oriented view; it talked not of elimination but upgrading of informal settlements, and introduced the idea of *in situ* improvements rather than building entirely new settlements and razing the slums to the ground. Housing policy was brought into line, according to the experts, with international best practice. The department was later renamed the Department of Human Settlement, signifying a shift to providing full and integrated settlements and not just rows of one-size-fits-all houses.

This approach, President Zuma said, 'is not just about building houses. It is also about transforming our residential areas and building communities with closer access to work and social amenities, including sports and recreation facilities'. Minister Sexwale, mixing his new-found knowledge of housing with his talent for rhyme and alliteration, said human settlements '… must be places where people play, stay and pray. They should be green, landscaped communities – pleasant places where people live, learn and have leisure.'

Policy had changed, but practice didn't. What we saw in the period after this were gigantic model projects, like Cosmo City not far from Diepsloot and the N2 Gateway project in the Western Cape, one in each province. These introduced mixed settlements, but they scratched the surface in terms of scale and numbers. And they chewed up the budget. The government was a massive house-building machine, but it was a blunt instrument, and could not make the shifts that were demanded. The focus was still one house per stand, knock down one shack and put up one house. But that, Topham says, is 'an abdication of responsibility. It is too simplistic a response to the complex problem of using housing to improve the livelihoods of the poor.'

The overwhelming political pressure is to build houses and provide services and to do this in numbers and of a quality better than the apartheid government. So in 1994 the ANC promised houses for all, and in 2004 it promised to eradicate all informal settlements by 2014. But there is neither the land nor the funding to do this. These promises – and the expectation that everyone can get their turnkey matchbox house – have kept things on a path which bears little relation to what can realistically be done. The government, faced with the political problem of admitting that it could not deliver what was now expected, stayed broadly on the same path.

Joburg, according to Topham, has one of the best planning departments in the country. Every city, by law, has to have an Integrated Urban Development Plan, which pulls together all the elements of the city's development, such as transport, power and infrastructure. Part of this is a Spatial Development Framework, which describes the spatial form of urban trends and the infrastructure which serves this. These are five-year plans, but they have to be reviewed and updated annually. They have to be approved by the MEC for local and provincial government and should drive the spending plans. It is intended to integrate national and local spending plans and development needs. Joburg has one of the best sets of such plans and frameworks: clear, simple, well-thought-through.

Implementation is another issue. Topham puts his finger on two issues to explain it: first, the lack of coordination between city departments working in silos; and second, the complex allocation/division of provincial and city powers and responsibilities.

In the early years of democracy, the city administration went through a radical modernisation and restructuring in which each service delivery arm – the electricity, water, refuse removal, gas and transport departments – was carved off into independent companies, known collectively as City-Owned Enterprises (COEs). In addition, they created the Joburg Development Agency, which would specialise in implementing any particular project given to it by the city, such as the rehabilitation of the city centre, the development of the Newtown Cultural Precinct, or the building of economic development nodes in Diepsloot. This allowed each COE to have a corporate structure, free from some structures of public service and city government and able to control its own hierarchy and budgets. They could be clearly accountable for what was expected of them and enjoy their financial and project management.

Co-ordination, though, is a nightmare. Now they have more silos than a Free State farming cooperative and getting them all to operate and implement, in harmony, is extremely difficult. The new Diepsloot Development Forum is intended to share information and coordinate planning, but it is too early to know how this will help.

The other problem, Topham says, is the division of powers of the province and the city, as set out in the constitution. The provinces have to submit plans for their share of the national budget for housing, and they get a three-year allocation, in line with the government's medium-term budgeting. This gives them a measure of stability and predictability, allowing for medium-term planning. But they make only a one-year budget commitment to cities, letting them know only on a year-to-year basis what they will have to spend. Consider that most service delivery projects have a minimum 18-month cycle and an *in situ* upgrade is a 3–5 year plan, and you can see that there is a problem.

The province also decides who implements, approves projects and has control of the product – even though the work is being done at a city level. Critical decisions like how to spend the subsidy (on project management, or just construction, or services?)

or who pays for what (should the city pay for the underground services?) were being made by politicians at some distance from implementation. So when the MEC for Housing was Nomvula Mokonyane, she did not encourage high-density housing, ignoring the land pressure. She is now provincial premier and estimates are that the province will run out of well-located available land in 2015.

In recent months, there have been shifts. The government has authorised the city itself to implement housing, rather than the province alone, which means that Diepsloot will sit firmly within the city's responsibility. Minister Sexwale is shifting to implement the policy changes, which have stood dormant for so long, though it is still impossible to admit that the government can't achieve the 'houses for all' promise. Deadlines for eradicating informal settlements are moving realistically outwards. Sexwale is also top-slicing 20 per cent of the housing budget for priority areas, and Diepsloot is one of them.

'Diepsloot does not have a champion. It needs something like the Alexandra Renewal Project (where a huge five-year grant was given to a special structure to tackle Alex's problems). It needs someone who can coordinate and implement a comprehensive plan for the area, and for money to be pumped in,' says Topham.

People remember that Joburg's Mayor Masondo set out in the beginning of his term to pave every road in Soweto. It took 10 years and it was done – a formidable achievement in overcoming a huge backlog – and it made a huge difference to that area. Now Diepsloot needs someone to champion it that way, to make sure it is treated as a priority and gets the money to make it happen.

Back to Diepsloot for a consultative meeting where city officials will present their plans. It is mid-week and late-afternoon, and the community hall holds about 40 people from the ANC, the ANC Youth League, Sanco, churches, traders' organisations and ward committees. Councillor Maele opens the meeting and fills in the background: a previous meeting had been briefed on plans to build houses in Diepsloot East and there was dispute over the sports fields demanded by some members of the community, because the space set aside for these took the place of about 200 houses. An earlier meeting had identified sports fields as a priority, particularly as the one soccer field had been lost to a new school building, causing some distress. But many had felt that houses were the priority, so the city planners had been sent back to find a way to incorporate the fields without losing any houses. They had come today to present their ideas.

André van der Walt, head of the planning team, says they have come up with a solution and he has a detailed display for them to see and communicate to their constituencies. The new plan will involve 7 260 houses, of which 5 000 will be semi-detached RDP houses. Along the roads, there will be 1 000 rental units in three-storey buildings and the balance will be for 'bond houses', bank-financed middle-class housing. There will be two RDP apartment buildings, and open spaces and parks for recreation. 'We are not going to compromise the quality of the houses, we are looking at improving it,' he says. He wants agreement that day to move ahead on this plan.

Maele says there needs to be consensus on the way forward. 'Because this development will take place during my term of office, I do not want to be blamed for rushing you into agreeing this setup.'

Questions flow about the size of the stands, the number of churches, accommodation for informal traders, and location of petrol stations. The central concerns are about the balance between the demand for housing and the need for space for commerce, green areas, sports and other facilities. The authorities want to create integrated living and communal areas, but residents want houses. For the politicians, timing is crucial: 'We have promised our people houses on this development going to the

2009 elections and now we are approaching the local elections in 2011, are they supposed to use the same plot again?' says Abram Mabuke, ward chair of the SACP and ANC secretary.

He is told that: 'The only thing delaying us was the agreement from the community and yourselves. But it might take about three, six or nine months pending the approval of the application for the establishment of a township.'

Van der Walt is telling them when his plan will be ready, holding out hope that it will start before the 2011 local government elections, avoiding the fact that the politicians still have to do their bit and find the money to do it.

Letsoalo, the controversial Sanco leader, rounds things off: 'We thank André and his team for this presentation. It looks beautiful, like a small cottage settlement in Fourways, and it will definitely assist in dealing with crime in the area. We are grateful for the 5 000 RDP units dedicated to the poor.'

Councillor Maele says he will write a letter of endorsement on behalf of the people of Diepsloot.

This is deliberative development at work, and Diepsloot has a history of it. Early on, the community formed the Community Development Forum (CDF), which represented residents and negotiated with the authorities for the first round of housing and services. It was sometimes divided, and had some bitter internal conflicts, but played a significant role in the early years in influencing what the province did for the area. In time, local elections were held and ward councillors elected to represent the area. The new local government law also created ward committees which the authorities were obliged to consult, and the councillors made the CDF redundant by agreeing only to deal with the official committees. Everyone I spoke to, including the councillors, agreed that the ward committees had become ineffectual.

Nevertheless, every development project goes through a consultative process and contractors appoint community liaison officers to handle relations throughout the process. This city meeting was notable in that it sought to resolve competing interests in how the land was divided up between houses, businesses, sports and parks. But the timeframes given to the community were unrealistic: the councillor said it would happen in the nine months he still had in office, and the planner said it would take up to nine months. Either they did not know that there was no budget allocated to it yet, or they were just playing for time.

The process is consultative, I notice, but it is not participative. It is still top-down. Residents vote every five years, and then wait to see whether the elected officials and their bureaucrats come and deliver to them. Officials consult the residents, and politicians visit and listen, but they are not harnessing the labour and desire for improved living conditions into active participation in anything other than asking them to come to occasional meetings. Residents and their political and home-grown structures are passive recipients of delivery. The ANC branch has created a forum to discuss development projects, and it works to ensure that delivery is efficient, open and fair. Mainly, they watch that their councillors are not favouring family and friends.

Interviewing politicians and city officials, we talk all the time, I realise, about whether service delivery is fast or slow. The problem is defined as one of delivery, never mind that the state may not have the human and financial resources to deliver what they are promising. It is like a pizza service without a motorbike. Or a pizza service where someone has dismantled the motorbike and given each part of the engine to a different company to fix.

We don't say that the problem is that you have unemployed labour and money and a need for houses, and you can't seem to put these things together to solve the problem. People build their own shacks, but you can't seem to get them to build their own houses. In fact, you discourage them from even improving their shacks by giving them a sense that they are in a temporary situation, that if they wait long enough they should get a house.

Who will build a house when someone else is offering to do

it? Who will improve a shack when it could get knocked down next week? And when you get a house, if you rent out space or try and turn it into an income-earning opportunity, you are reprimanded. Rather wait, you are being told, and we will create jobs and deliver houses.

Rather wait.

When I ask for an interview, Mayor Amos Masondo sets up a show for me. He is a solid and uncorrupted but dour and uncharismatic politician and therefore is well advised to bring in a bevy of smart young officials and other politicians to give me a series of presentations on how the city is tackling its informal areas. Meeting in his plush chambers in Braamfontein, central Joburg, they project colourful maps on to the wall and hand out lengthy council reports written in the tortured language of bureaucracy.

The city, Mayor Masondo says, is prioritising informal settlements – and since Diepsloot is one of the biggest, it is high up on their list. Councillor Roslynn Greef, the management committee member for development planning and urban management, talks of an 'intense focus on marginalised areas'. The formidably named Informal Settlement Formalisation and Upgrading Steering Committee have listed and categorised the settlements they are tackling and have set out to barcode each shack, though they have managed only to do about a third of them.

First the committee members have to understand the legal and zoning status of the land, and confirm who owns it, which can be complicated. The majority of these settlements are on unsuitable land, and a number are on private property and face eviction. They have identified 23 settlements they can tackle first, and are now developing basic layout plans and a register of occupants to establish what services and facilities are needed. Each settlement has to be registered as a township and a township register drawn up. Then they will draw up business plans for each one. This is intended to be done within two years – a formidable task just to get their heads around the nature and scale of the project. It has already taken two years, with R20-million spent in year one and R30-million set aside for year two.

They give me an honest outline of the issues and challenges and it sounds overwhelming: Joburg has 182 informal settlements involving 180 000 households. That's the official figure. One can expect it to get higher, and it is growing all the time. Fifty-nine settlements have to be relocated, which means land has to be found or acquired and the difficult process of getting people to move has to be undertaken. Eighteen are on private land, totalling just under 1 000 hectares. While they plan capital projects to upgrade these areas, they also have to continue with maintenance of existing services.

The mayor, though, is firm that with application, determination and imagination, it can be done. 'When I went to parliament and said we were going to pave every road in Soweto, they told me I was mad. It is done,' he says. He also compares the situation to US President John Kennedy saying in 1968 that they would land a man on the moon. 'Many people thought he was crazy, including the scientists working on it. But it had to be done. We dare not give up.'

Nobody can quite put their finger on the time scale or where the money will come from. They have hope, a determined optimism, and impressive plans. But Diepsloot has to fight for attention and resources against 181 other Diepsloots. Most of them are not as big, but they are equally complex and difficult.

Oh, and Councillor Greef throws in one other thing: in Diepsloot, there is also the problem of The Frog. There will have to be a conservation area and an education centre to turn the troublesome beast into a local asset.

CHAPTER NINE

'Anything you need, it is here'

Diepsloot buzzes with retail activity. At the side of every street, down every nook and cranny, there is someone selling something to make a living. The chain stores are in the Mall, perched on the edge of the area, and spread all around are a few large and formal shops and taverns, but smaller structures are the rule, with shipping containers, shacks and sometimes just pole and tarpaulin structures housing every kind of enterprise from hairdressers to internet cafés.

There are even more streetside or backyard traders with nothing more than a sunshade in an open space, selling cigarettes, sweets and a few vegetables, or hawking electrical goods, sneakers or clothing. There are savvy street hustlers touting medicinal concoctions and HIV cures. 'You can buy anything next to the road in Diepsloot,' I am repeatedly told. 'Anything you need, it is here.' Most of it is the urban equivalent of the peasant making just enough to keep going, not enough to build a business or develop stock. It is survivalist trade, not more than that, and it is abundant.

When I interview street traders, I am struck by how little money most of them make. There are too many selling the same stuff at similar prices, and many buy their goods from 'the Indians' in the city or even within Diepsloot and then resell them in another part of the settlement. This means that both volumes and margins are tiny.

Joe Thema, 43, lives in Extension 10 and has done so since 1996, with his wife and three children. For three years he has sold peanuts, snuff, cigarettes and crisps from his yard, to supplement the money his wife brings in from piece jobs. He buys his goods in bulk from 'Indians in Randburg' and makes his profit by selling in smaller quantities, so a packet of *amaskopas* (coloured popcorn) costs R13 and he sells packets of it for 50c; or a large packet of peanuts costs him R30 and he breaks it into R1 packs. When business is good he can make R40 a day, but his biggest problem is having enough cash to buy stock. He often has to borrow to stock up, he says.

Nelson Mazuze moved to the Reception Area from Alex in 2002, and rented a place in Extension 10 a year ago to start his business. Partially disabled by a leg injury, he began by selling sweets from his wheelchair. Now he sells facecloths, belts, dresses, wallets and cigarettes, most of which he buys from a shop in central Johannesburg. He will buy a pack of cigarettes for R20 and sell them for R2 each – a 100 per cent profit. The margins on clothing are smaller: a R12 cap sells for between R15 and R20. Turnover depends on the time of the month: mid-month he will take R150 to R200 a day, and this will double at the end of the month. He ends up with about R1 000 at the end of most weeks, and as much as R5 000 around Christmas time. He is fortunate in that his landlords are flexible: he sometimes pays them R100, sometimes R200, depending on how things have been that month.

Elizabeth Mudau and her husband are minor landlords. They have an RDP house and rent out shacks on their property. Her children are at school in Venda. She runs a small shop on her property as well, but finds it hard because of the number of traders in her area, particularly foreigners who undercut her prices, she says. Some of her stock she buys from them and resells, otherwise she gets it in Marabastad, Pretoria. She sells fruit, vegetables, crisps and cigarettes and takes in only about R50–R70 per day.

Tsepo Podile has a larger business, a hair salon which he runs from a container. He pays R400 a month for the container and R300 for his shack in Extension 8. The salon brings in R1 200 to R1 800 a week from hairdos at between R40 and R70, depending on what products they want used, and selling products bought in bulk and decanted into smaller containers. His biggest problem is not enough customers, as there are many salons in the area.

Brian Mazibuko has only been in Diepsloot for a few months, and came from KwaZulu-Natal. His stall is on the street, so he pays no rent and takes out about R2 000 a week. He sells a range of goods – from dishcloths to paraffin stoves and playing cards – with small mark-ups. His biggest problem, he says, is people stealing from his stall.

Keaobaka Sekukuna has a more specialised shop, dealing only in cigarettes and Rizla rolling papers for tobacco. She comes from Mafikeng, in North West province, and has been doing this for three months in the same spot in the street, because there she does not need to pay rent. She buys cartons from the local mall or from 'Indian shops' and sells individual cigarettes for between R1 and R2, depending on the brand, taking home about R120 a day.

A few traders tell me that they have to pay someone to keep their spot. Sipho Ndlovu, a Zimbabwean who has been trading for only about three months, says Metro Police came around and demanded R60. 'I paid them R40,' he says, and was told to expect them to come around every six months.

Precious Ndlovu, from Zimbabwe, has been trading for about a year. She says she is made to pay R10 every now and then, but is also not sure of who she is paying nor why. 'We are called to the ranks and we pay R10 each. I've only been here for two months, so I don't know when the next time to pay will be. They'll probably just call us again.'

The lunchtime launch in one of Diepsloot's community halls of the Traders' Forum gets off to a slow start with about 50 people present. But disparate groups of people of all ages wander in over the next hour, until about 200 are packed in. This forum is one of a number being set up as part of the plan to launch Dicob, the Diepsloot Chamber of Business. There is a long agenda: a keynote political speech by the Sanco chair, a host of messages of support from all sorts of organisations – from the Metro Police to the Foreign Traders' Forum, launched just a week earlier as part of the same process – and the election of a committee. The mood is one of chaotic, informal democracy, held together by goodwill and common interest. The leadership sit at the front, behind a table with a floral cloth, biscuits, glasses and two-litre cold-drink bottles in a neat row, provided by the representative of the Foreign Traders' Forum. Sitting to one side is a row of special guests – local authority representatives, politicians, Absa bank officials and myself, the sole journalist.

The forums are being launched and will be pulled together into the chamber to deal with the tensions between local and foreign traders. Lucas Loate, who had been commissioned by one arm of the ANC to run with this initiative, had seen that to do it, one had to deal with the frustrations of the local traders. So the chamber will not only bring together the locals and foreigners to bash out understandings, but seek to address those factors that are giving the foreigners the edge over the locals – bulk buying and enjoying credit, essentially.

The keynote speaker from Sanco was Letsoalo, the man who had told me he would only speak when there was money on the table. I learnt for the first time that his name was Phineas Letsoalo Senior, and he kicked off the meeting with a rousing, populist attack on the banks who had no regard for the small traders. They were the outsiders coming in, and they would need to be taught to answer to local needs and demands. They were the foreigners to worry about. He promised that they would force the banks to start loaning money to the traders.

I turned to the local representatives of Absa, South Africa's biggest bank and part of the international Barclays Group, who were sitting next to me. They shrugged their shoulders and said they could only talk about the new product they had come to offer. I asked if they often had to deal with the politics and they said: 'We only deal with individuals. And our products.'

Letsoalo turned to the issue of foreign residents, and he dealt with the anti-xenophobia message in an unexpected way. Some foreigners, he said, came to work here and they were legal and had papers and they were welcome, while others came to fight and commit crime, and 'we' would fight with them. But, he said, when you have a fight with a foreign trader, 'don't call others to fight with you. Go and sort it out with that person.'

With that, he called on everyone to join the ANC so that they could be part of the coming local government elections. And this was telling: his message was not to register as a voter, but to register as a branch member. The battle, he was indicating, is about who the candidate will be, rather than the actual vote. To influence this, you had to be a branch member.

He was followed by his son, Phineas Letsoalo Junior, whose contribution was less populist, more practical and less rhetorical. He said the new business chamber would try and bring people together to create economies of scale. They would open common accounts with suppliers which would serve their members and give them the weight of collective scale. They would also assist with 'issues of compliance' – getting the traders to legalise themselves. 'These will be the first steps to alleviate poverty,' he said.

When I sit down in a council office to talk to Lucas Loate I start with a couple of what have become my standard opening questions, which serve to get people to relax and open up: 'How long have you been in Diepsloot? What brought you here? Lucas's answer takes about 30 minutes. It is told in great detail in an expressionless monotone, with no sense of rancour or bitterness.

Lucas is impeccably dressed in a neatly pressed suit, with a pink open-necked shirt. He is a slim, elegant man, but what stands out is his shiny gold shoes, a pair I was to often see on him, a badge of distinction.

Lucas was in Grade 10 when he came to Diepsloot from Pretoria in 1994, making him one of the original residents. His mother was a domestic worker in the area and had found a shack in Extension 1, so he joined her there. He was the oldest child; his siblings stayed with an aunt. From the way he tells it, it is clear he has a strong sense of family. He started Grade 11 in a local farm school recently taken over by the government. He had a passion and aptitude for maths and science and his heart was set on becoming a doctor.

Poorly advised, he failed to get the matric credits he needed to go to university, so he went to a private college in town, wrote his matric again and got the results he wanted and needed. But three years of frustration followed, as he applied for and failed to get every possible bursary or scholarship to study medicine. In the meantime, he taught at a local education centre, giving extra lessons in his favourite subjects of maths and science.

Then he hit it lucky: his mother now had a job with a French family and they offered to assist him if he got himself accepted into a medical school. That year he applied and gained admission into both the University of the Witwatersrand and Medunsa medical schools. 'But they left the country and went back to France, and that was that,' he says. The end of his medical ambitions.

But not the end of his ambitions. 'I kept on motivating my-self,' he says. 'My house was like a classroom, teaching students on weekends and during holidays.' He started an informal school, drawing in friends of his who were skilled but unemployed. They had two classes going, and an agreement with a local school which let them use facilities and gave them basics like chalk to use.

Then he landed a job as a gardener, through a contact he made in church. 'Apparently, I did a good job, because they were paying R80 per day, but after three days they gave me R500.' Then came a painting job for a Mozambican, at R50 per day, but that only lasted two months before the job was complete. He was still teaching at night and on weekends.

Then he had another break. Someone told him that Absa was recruiting and he should put his CV in at the city councillor's office. 'There were too many CVs, so I thought I would never make it. Then they called me and I was lucky because then I had this old cellphone I had found in a taxi and you had to charge it the whole day. I left it to charge and when I came back there was a message saying I should be there the next day. I went and they took us to the Department of Labour. Again, there were too many people: 400 people interviewing for 60 jobs.'

His tale mixes luck with the strength of his forceful personality. He was ambitious and determined, but he makes it clear that there were lucky breaks along the way, like getting tipped off about jobs, or getting cellphone messages just in time. But he has also had his share – more than his fair share – of bad turns.

'There was a three-level screening process, and you had to go through each one. But during the first interview, they went outside for a bit and came back and said I don't have to go through the whole thing because they will definitely put me in the programme. I was so excited to share that news with my family. We were in a one-room shack and I was happy because I could see my mother and brother every day.' There was more good fortune: his mother was allocated an RDP house and they moved in.

He reported for duty at Absa and was put in a year-long training programme to introduce people to banking. 'I could hold my own. It was all about corporate etiquette and I could not understand why we were doing this. At the end of the year, management came and said they would be offering some contracts. I was given a position as a consultant in telephone and internet banking.' That was in 2005; in 2006 he was made a team leader, and in 2007 a team co-ordinator. In that time, he married and had a son, and built his mother 'the kind of house I wished for her to have'. His wife was at university and was trying to find a job. They rented a townhouse.

Then the next blow: 'Absa said they were doing away with our division and I had to leave. I was retrenched.' He was stuck with the townhouse lease for a while, but when it ran out they had to move back to Diepsloot. Fortunately, the additional room he had built for his mother made it easier to share her three-bedroomed house, with a brother in the yard shack. He has since been employed as a regional project manager for a community work programme, a job-creation scheme which employs about 500 people to clear crime spots and build ways to cross the river, and is staying in Fourways.

In Diepsloot, he became involved in politics. 'I had always had the interest, but it was then that I was introduced to it and joined [the ANC].' One day in early 2010, a complaint was brought to a councillor he was working with about foreign business owners opening shops everywhere in the area and undercutting prices. 'The councillor came to me to assist and I spent about a week studying it, and had to come up with a strategy to try and integrate the two [local and foreign business people].

'When I spoke to people about it, I realised that it was not these people [the foreigners] who were the problem. It was that the local guys did not have the skill to compete with them. They [the foreigners] were offering things cheaper because they were buying bulk and able to drop prices because they were selling quantity.

'They have these communities, Pakistanis and so on, where they all buy at one place, they open one big account, so they get things cheaper, they use economy of scale.

'So I realised that someone had to take responsibility to educate our people. Also, it seemed like a tuck shop was the only business they [the locals] could do. When I went and talked to them, I heard business ideas, but they didn't know how to do it.

'And there were finance issues. People did not have the finance to build their businesses.'

He told the councillor to give him another two weeks and he would go and talk to the foreign businessmen as well. 'You see, there were also unfair business practices – they would open two shops on either side of a business, and squeeze them out. I said this is not doing you or our cause any good.'

He decided to create a forum to bring together local and foreign business. For the foreigners, he would encourage them to be 'socially responsible', and make it 'easier for them to be accepted'. He also talked to them about 'their responsibility to help our people'. Larger enterprises would call it corporate social investment.

There were other business problems to be tackled in Diepsloot. 'I learnt that the ANC branch was divided into two. The issue was that they [the leadership] all had contractor companies and they all wanted jobs. The councillor would give one a contract and then they would mobilise against him. When they toyi-toyied, they said it was about service delivery, but really it was personal.

'People from other areas would know there was a tender and would win it, because our leadership was not focused, we would miss it, even though we had some skills. For example, the school they are building, that's a R16-million project. One guy comes here, he wins the tender, he brings his own labour, and nobody questions this. Often they don't do a quality job; he got it because he is a comrade. He takes everything, and the labour gets nothing. I am of the view that development should create jobs here; there should be skills development, it must benefit this community.

'In addition, we have guys who run hardware businesses here, but these contractors buy from outside. Why can't they support the guys here?

'I also found that our contractors don't know how to quote, so they only take sub-contracts and never the tender itself, the main contract.'

Lucas thought the place needed a business chamber – a place where all of these issues could be dealt with. 'I did a lot of consulting. It posed a threat to some, because there already was a plan to launch another regional business body, the Noweto Chamber. A couple of people tried to fight us, but we had a consultation process so we could survive that storm.'

He also pulled in outside help – a senior man from Anglo American who lived in Fourways, a legal adviser from the Development Bank, and other professionals. They registered a Section 21 company, the Diepsloot Chamber of Commerce, and formed a board. 'We had to have people who live and run businesses in Diepsloot, as well as some tried and tested people who bring value.'

He first got each business sector in Diepsloot to form their own forum – a construction forum, hawkers, informal traders, security, catering, hair salons, transport and then the Foreign Traders' Forum, which in turn was made up of a Pakistani forum and a Somali forum. 'The Ethiopians are not organised,' he says; they seem to keep their heads down. Now he is preparing to launch the overarching chamber which will bring these forums together.

He spoke to the banks. 'Where we put our account, they must see us not as a client, but as a partner. There is a need for loans now, and some of the conditions were very steep. They said they would relax their conditions if we do training.' They went to the Development Bank for support, and opened a conversation with the developers of Dainfern, the nearby high-income area, where they were planning to build a very large surrounding wall (probably to keep out the people of Diepsloot). 'We told them they must use our people. They had been running into battles over the politics – and this was scaring them off. We said we will deal with the politics, and you deal with us.'

Lucas is now working major time organising the forum. It is voluntary work with just a small budget to run an office in his mother's garage. The political battles are substantial, and have clearly taken a toll on him. He is dismissive of the rival chamber 'because these guys do not even live in Diepsloot', though they own taverns, and just want to secure work for themselves, he says. But they have money and power and influence in the ANC and he faces resistance from ANC leaders who are 'holding on to their power'.

Ironically, he has found support in Sanco. 'Sanco has power here, they are stronger than the ANC and have stronger leadership by a long way. These guys are influential. They team up with the SACP and the ANC Youth League and they go and take on the membership of the ANC. At an ANC meeting, they are the majority.'

At one point, he was summoned to the city regional director's office where a Development Bank representative held a meeting with both chambers, and told them they had to get together. But the other group, he says, have no status and no papers. After the hard-fought 2010 battle over ANC provincial leadership, some of the established businessmen took him to a tavern to celebrate. One of them said they knew he was unemployed and asked how much they should pay him to drop his chamber plans. 'I told him I was not somebody who can just be bought. He apologised, and asked to meet our board. I told him to write me a letter, and it never came.'

In ANC branch documents later I find a resolution denouncing Lucas's chamber. An ANC official tells me that they back the rival effort, and that Lucas's efforts are 'seriously counter-revolutionary'.

The local, internal political and resource rivalries pollute everything.

A sign along Ingonyama Road catches my eye: Diepsloot Cinema. I follow an arrow down a side road to one of the few industrial-type buildings in the area and meet Emanuel, who rents the building from a friend.

Emanuel came from Polokwane in 2002 in search of work. He had not finished school, but got himself onto a three-month course in Alex on repairing and maintaining generators and then came to set up an operation in Diepsloot. His main business is fixing and renting out all sorts of equipment, mostly generators and lawnmowers, which takes up only one of the three rooms in his rented premises, so he put a cinema into another and a pool table into the third.

The cinema is low-tech stuff: about 30 plastic chairs are lined up in a room, one wall is painted white and a data projector is precariously suspended to one side, propped up by books and magazines. There is a popcorn machine and home-drawn movie adverts along the other walls. Emanuel is vague about where he gets his films, but he says he shows mainly action movies on weekends. He started off charging R3 for a film, but found that it was too expensive for people, so now he charges R2 for adults and R1 for kids, who are most of his clientele. But he found he could charge R3 for big soccer matches and get packed houses. He also makes a bit from selling sweets and popcorn.

Emanuel knows what he has to do to grow his business. He has to get more equipment to rent out, he has to buy a bakkie so that he can fetch and deliver stuff in Fourways and other surrounding areas, and he needs to buy his own pool table, as the one he has is owned by someone else and he has to share the income from it. Sounds to me like he has a sound sense of business strategy, and he is one of very few business people in the area doing something other than straightforward retail. So what is holding him up? He needs capital and 'I don't know how to get it.'

Emanuel's businesses are not registered, and he works out of a personal bank account. I tell him that to get a loan he will need to get legitimate, but this makes him nervous: 'I am not very literate. I will have to do forms, and tax and all sorts of things …' It is clear that he feels out of his depth thinking about how to put his business on a proper basis. But he wants to do it. I put him in touch with an operation that specialises in assisting people like Emanuel to take their businesses forward.

As much as financial capital, Emanuel lacks the social capital for his business – and this is something I find in numerous encounters around Diepsloot. Although he clearly has a business nose, he does not have the knowledge, contacts or network to find finance. To do so, he would have to register his business, run a proper set of books, sort out his tax … which would cost him a lot before he gets the benefits, and which he is nervous to do. Even suggesting he goes down this path feels like sending him into a high-risk area. It is easy to see why small business so often stays small business.

Lucas Loate's push to start the Diepsloot Chamber of Commerce is pre-empted by his rivals: the Noweto Chamber of Commerce and Industry is launched at the Diepsloot Mall on 22 October 2010. The split reflects the ANC–Alliance division. Lucas has been working with Councillor Maele and clearly has a relationship with Sanco. The Noweto Chamber features Councillor Ndlazi and ANC chair Rogers Makhubele. It is also a class split: Dicob is an organisation largely of small and informal traders struggling to make a living, while

Noweto represents the bigger, formal businesses – all the talk is of 'becoming millionaires'.

At the Noweto launch, Ndlazi promises the support of the City of Johannesburg, which 'would also like to invest in the chamber to further promote and support local entrepreneurs'. He describes the area as 'formerly under-privileged' and challenges the chamber to be inclusive, to incorporate the businesses of KyaSands and Fourways, and even get together with the wealthy areas of Hyde Park and Sandton. His dream is of a regional chamber which will put them all under one roof – a grander vision and purpose than Loate's, whose focus has been very much on Diepsloot's needs, on the smaller trader.

'With this launch,' Diepsloot resident and chair of the National Hawkers Association, Betuel Nomavuka, says, 'we are transforming ourselves [from] being informal traders to formal businesses. We don't have to sit around and complain that government is not doing anything for us, but what we are doing for ourselves and the country.'

Rather mysteriously, he calls on the councillors whose term is coming to an end to prepare to join the chamber. 'The time for stomach politics is over, come to the business sector to become millionaires and billionaires. At Noweto we talk about business not politics, stand up and make sure that you do something for yourself.'

Chamber president Lucky Moshimane has a simple message: 'We are tired of being sub-contractors, we must become main contractors. I am saying it is time for us to unite, and fight for our rights. My goal is to see our members becoming millionaires during my term of office.'

Another speaker, introduced only as MacDonald, is more modest: 'The main purpose of business is to make money, some might become millionaires but the point is that everyone should make money.'

And one, introduced only as Zama, has a special message for

the youth: 'Our youth must learn to become employers because we are tired of being employed.'

There are also speeches from the president of the Junior Chamber of Commerce International and a representative of Nafcoc, the national black chamber of commerce.

At 3 pm, lunch is served. This is a long way from the container in the Reception Area where I saw local and foreign traders thrash out an agreement.

The key man in this Noweto chamber is Lucky Moshimane. His is the archetypal informal settlement success story: he is a hugely successful business figure, proud of having made his first million in Diepsloot. He is an icon, a Diepslooter who started with nothing and dealt his way out of poverty by making and taking opportunities. I first come across him when people point to a string of shops, taverns, a butchery and a funeral parlour in Extension 2 and tell me they belong to 'Lucky the Diepsloot millionaire', with a sense of awe. He then emerges as the chair of the Noweto Chamber of Business and publisher of the new *Noweto News* newspaper.

I try to speak to Moshimane. His personal assistant says she will come back to me. She messages: 'Mr Moshimane's lawyer will be contacting you shortly.' He doesn't – and further queries and notes meet with silence. Fortunately, Phillip Makwela, the ANC Youth League leader who also runs www.diepsloot.com, gives me an interview and profile he has done with Moshimane.

Moshimane was one of the original residents, having come from Zevenfontein in early 1995 where most people were ANC-aligned. They moved into the Rhema block in the Resettlement Camp, where there were many IFP members, and this led to conflict which burst into violence in 1995/6. Moshimane played a key role as an ANC Youth League leader and was then anointed ANC chair in Diepsloot 'by the ANC elders'. He set up the first anti-crime vigilante unit, Mapogo a Mathamaga, which became notorious for a very rough justice. 'The business and community shield' it called itself, offering 'guarding service at very affordable tariffs'.

During his term of office, Moshimane dealt with taxi violence between rival associations jockeying for the territory, and he facilitated negotiations to bring them together into a new, united taxi body. He led a number of ANC protests, including ones calling for an end to taxi fighting and in pursuit of the formal declaration of Diepsloot as a township, at a time when their legal status was uncertain and they were viewed by the farm owner as squatters. Notably, he led a march to the Randburg council offices and another to the home of Nelson Mandela. He claims credit for creating a system to stem the flow of people into Diepsloot and make the area safe, pushing for Extension 2 to be formalised into stands for residents, and introducing a bus service when the taxi wars were a problem.

In 1996, he left the ANC to pursue his business interests, and has flourished in the short time since then. But he is very proud of his role in and links with the ANC. 'I started the ANC in Diepsloot and Zevenfontein ... and I have been arrested in the process,' he told Phillip.

He began with a butchery, now called Hlope's, sold that and opened the Mississippi Tavern. When Tokyo Sexwale was provincial premier, he challenged him to come to Diepsloot. 'Tokyo ate lunch in my pub,' he says proudly. Now he runs much bigger businesses – Jamba Security, Afri-Eagle Construction and Tsogo Funerals. Jamba's website says it is 'a proudly BLACK BROAD BASED EMPOWERMENT EQUITY' and its founding partners, Moshimane and Kefilwe Mkono, are 'committed, ambitious and disciplined individuals' who formed the company in response to 'the outcry by various communities across the country who felt threatened'.

Afri-Eagle, he tells people, was inspired by what he learnt about building while still at school and working for his uncle, building houses in Dainfern, where he now lives. Moshimane is outspoken about empowerment and believes he is different to other employers of Diepsloot people. 'Most of the business people in the north are exploiting Diepsloot people because they are not educated. My businesses empower people,' he has said. 'Diepsloot is a target for cheap labour. Just look around in the morning and evenings, you will see bakkies carrying a lot of people who are used by people in the north to get rich.'

He is president of the Noweto Business Chamber; late in 2010 he also launched *Noweto News*, a local paper. Using the name 'Noweto' takes it beyond Diepsloot into the wider field he is now ploughing, making the settlement part of the wider and flourishing regional economy and evoking an old apartheid name dating back to a government plan in the 1980s to create a northern Soweto, Noweto, in the area.

'My main concern is that we have teachers, doctors, entrepreneurs and brilliant people in Diepsloot. Yet, the only picture the media see about Diepsloot is negative. They are tarnishing our area just because they want to gain something. I am the child of Diepsloot soil,' he pointed out to Phillip.

A close look at his companies indicates that most of their work is for the province and city. They offer a range of industrial, commercial, residential and VIP protection services, but notably also 'relocation of informal settlements', 'management of informal settlements' and 'relocation of eviction victims' – ironic specialisations for someone who was himself a victim of eviction and relocation, and the product of an informal settlement. Indeed, he found himself caught in controversy when managing an eviction from River Glen, not far from Diepsloot. 'Lucky was accused of betraying the residents because they claimed he promised together with the developer to find alternative accommodation and encouraged them to sign up for the RDP houses being offered,' I am told.

His businesses overlap. In the River Glen case, after Jamba

Security moved people, his Afri-Eagle Construction was the main contractor on the development, Jamba provided the security, and he was project manager.

Jamba boasts of having relocated over 10 000 people on behalf of the city. This includes, their website says, relocations 'from Zeverfontein to Cosmo-City, Zamimpilo informal settlement to Pennyville Housing Project, Doornkop informal settlement to Doornkop Housing Project, Honeydew informal settlement internal relocation, Kaya-Sands informal settlement internal relocation, Kaya-Sands flood-line internal relocation, Diepsloot informal settlement to Adelaide Tambo settlement.' In other words, he handles the difficult people movements in the region, those that require knowledge of the politics of informal settlements backed by brute force, a combination he clearly offers.

While talking to ANC leaders, I learn also that he is a major contributor to and sponsor of the local party and its officials. When Rogers Makhubele is awaiting election to the council, ANC provincial chair and political fixer Paul Mashatile arranges for Moshimane to put him on the payroll for a few months. Moshimane has also said to those around him that he gave Councillor Maele up to R200 000 and bought him a car, only to fall out with him later because Maele wanted his brothers to be sub-contractors on a big job.

What emerges is a triangular relationship of mutual patronage between Moshimane, the local ANC and the state structures which dish out tenders and contracts. As a wealthy ANC supporter, Moshimane supports the local party and its officials. He wins provincial and city contracts to move people, provide security and build on a large scale. He can then offer sub-contracts and jobs to Diepsloot people, and is under pressure to give them to those with political connections.

Is this corruption? It is certainly clientelism and political patronage of the kind that is common in local governments across the world, but does it cross a line into buying favours and paying for contracts? Moshimane will argue that it is of greater benefit to the people of Diepsloot if the contract goes to someone like him with close links to the place and its people, who spends as much of the money there as he can and employs as many locals as possible. The alternative would be a large outside firm which is likely to spend and employ outside, feeding little of the cash flow into the Diepsloot economy. Hence his rhetoric of empowerment. He would say that there is nothing wrong with making donations to the party, he does it with pride and gratitude for what it has enabled him to achieve. He might point to the alleged refusal to accommodate a councillor's family in the circle of benefit as a sign that he is not corrupt – he is not prepared to involve those who might not be able to do the work and deliver the goods. He would point to a meeting he called in January 2011 to discuss employing local youths on his project.

Trying to unravel these links, I wonder to what extent this is a legitimate part of the national project to build a black middle class, to close the income, skills and opportunities gap inherited from apartheid, to carry through the policy of restitutive affirmative action in the granting of government work? Is it successfully redistributive? If it costs a bit more, but feeds more of that money into Diepsloot, is this a reasonable exchange? Is this functional, even if it is borderline corruption?

Every time I drive into Diepsloot, I am struck by Ingonyama Road, the main thoroughfare which has been rebuilt many times and collapses repeatedly because it was never properly constructed. Even the people who laid the Government Precinct element of it, which is now a good road, tell me that when they dug up the old road, they found that the foundational engineering was faulty and they had to spend more than expected in doing it properly for the first time. And I see the police station standing half-complete. Is this the price of clientelism, of patronage, of the murky triangle of mutual benefit? To argue for a functional level of minor corruption is dangerous ground to tread if it leads to wholesale corruption of the sort that will mean these roads are never properly built, if it does not redistribute the benefits, if the police station is unduly delayed. Or if these relationships of patronage are the fuel that fires the bitter political rivalries and competitiveness.

The test, I tell myself, is whether the work gets done at reasonable cost and on deadline, and gets done properly. Does the project enhance the people of Diepsloot's trust in the system, or does it undermine it? It is clear that in this murky triangle Moshimane benefits, ANC leadership benefits, the local party benefits, as do its officials. What is less clear to me is whether the people of Diepsloot benefit.

CHAPTER TEN

'The people are too much and the needs are high'

A *Daily Sun* article alerted me to MaJacky. It had a picture of her with 40 street kids she had taken in and cared for. Her small RDP house was an unofficial, informal, Diepsloot children's haven.

The newspaper gave her phone number, but she was not hard to find. I drove around the area and adults and children alike all knew her and her house, pointing down the maze of roads that led to it. From the article, I expected to find a cheerful matron and teams of kids, but I found a depressed house, with only a few youngsters hanging around. Government social workers had been there just a few days before and taken away many of the kids, threatening to close down her haven.

Jacqueline Mkhubele, known as MaJacky, was born in Alex and came to Diepsloot in 1996 by the most tortured route imaginable – one that set her on the path of dedication to child-care. When she was very young, her grandmother had taken her from Alex to Mpumalanga, but had died suddenly – and, with no way of contacting her mother, Jacqueline was left to fend for herself and her younger sister. 'When you stay alone, you do what you like at that age. We didn't go to school, when we went next door, they told us to go away … I became a street kid then. I was smoking, drinking beer, going to the shebeen …

I just grew like that, and if some man wanted me, they just took me, I would have to sleep with that man.'

Another 'mama', who said she knew where Jacqueline came from in Alex, took her to Joburg and found her a job as a domestic worker and later at a supermarket. This woman took her to church and 'that was what changed me'. She stopped hanging out in taverns and drinking and smoking. One day, this 'mama' took her to Alex and showed her where she had lived in 15th Street. A woman recognised her and told her she knew her mother, Elsie. She took Jacqueline to what had been her mother's place – 'a big house, because my father was a boxer'. Her mother had run away, 'because my father had hit her', and her father was now with another woman. Her father, she says, asked her to sleep with him. 'I ran away, I became a street kid again.'

She heard that people were being moved to Diepsloot where they were going to get houses. 'I went to the truck with nothing. I didn't have a shack, I didn't have any papers, but I got on the truck and they brought me here [to Diepsloot Reception Area].'

The church gave her material to build a shack, as well as blankets and food. She did some small-time trading to keep herself going. 'Then I saw some kids who were not going to school or to crèche and they said their mother had passed away' – a story familiar to her. 'It hurt me to see these kids, and I said these kids have no mother and I haven't got kids. I can look after them.' She spoke to the local figure of authority, the ANC secretary, who encouraged her to take these children in, and told her that when she did not have food she should go round to the local shops and ask them for help. 'Another man who had a big shop gave me a roof to make a bigger shack.'

The shops would give her mealie meal which had been spoiled by rats and she would sift it and cook it. 'Lots of kids came. The church gave us clothes and things. It was the church that changed things,' she says, again.

In 2002, she was granted her RDP house and brought 10 kids with her. The house is on the south side of the settlement, near a rubbish dump. 'I saw children at the dump and they told me they came there to find food. I brought them here, fed them and they stayed. Children came from all over.' She shows me a picture of herself with 12 children of all ages.

Her house is comfortable and packed with furniture and bric-a-brac. The TV is playing continually. Pride of place goes to a wall of pictures of her and her children. There is a bookcase full of children's books. Her yard is cleared and covered in carpeting off-cuts for the kids to play on. She shows me the reed fence she has built to keep the yard safe. She pulls out a file to show me certificates for courses she has done in child care and development, with the help of various NGOs. She is brimming with pride. 'I tell these kids why I do it: because I didn't stay with my mum, I didn't get love from my mum, now I am your mum, I love you, I take you to church ...' She has joined the ZCC church and found some corporate support. An insurance company put a ceiling in her house. A major supermarket chain gives her potatoes, and another company fixed up her toilet. 'Now you see how nice it is – like one for white people,' she laughs.

When she needs money for the kids, she goes around the neighbourhood and people help her. One of her wards died just a few days ago from HIV/AIDS, she says in a matter-of-fact-way, and she will go round to ask for money to help bury the child. She has no doubt that she will get it.

Three months back, the government social workers came. 'They said I could not keep the kids like this, I would need to put a toilet outside, I must build an office, I must build a class-room outside. I couldn't keep more than six kids here. I had to have a health certificate. Everything will have to change – and they took my kids.' She closes her eyes and sobs, and I realise how fragile she is behind her straightforward demeanour. 'That was three months ago. She [the social worker] took 12 kids to Soweto. Now I don't even know if my kids are eating.'

It is a tale of the evolution of Diepsloot. MaJacky's set-up is typical of how people worked out informal solutions at a time when there were no structures, no rules and no official-dom in the informal settlement. But now there is a push by the authorities to bring law, order, regulation and control – and that involves insisting that people like her conform to standards and rules designed to protect children. But the transition is a difficult one, particularly for someone with few resources, and MaJacky is devastated. 'Why did she [the social worker] do it like this? She doesn't know this place. She doesn't love me. She doesn't love the kids.'

A few minutes later, she takes a deep breath and composes herself. She has a dream. Someone has shown her a piece of land she can use by the Hennops River. 'My hope is a swimming pool, a library, a computer system, a special classroom, a social workers' room, an office, all of this for my kids.' But mean-while, she has to find a way to fix up her place and get a health certificate, so that at least some of her kids can come home.

A large piece of Diepsloot land, tucked behind the Diepsloot Mall and fenced off, is owned by the Methodist Church. The church building and minister's house are there, but the grounds also house a private low-cost school – one of a few owned by a black educational entrepreneur, the makeshift offices of the city arts and culture project in a prefabricated building alongside a basketball court, and the MaAfrika Tikkun Centre, a large-scale community project started by wealthy philanthropist Bertie Lubner and former Chief Rabbi Cyril Harris, with Nelson Mandela as patron-in-chief. MaAfrika evokes the warm and strong image of African matriarchy, and Tikkun is a Hebrew word for change – together I hear them often abbreviated to MaTikkun.

The place is a hive of cheerful activity – kids playing in the school yard, kids from the MaTikkun Early Education Centre singing in a circle, a young girl teaching others to do what looks like American-style cheerleading, other children playing on a merry-go-round water pump, youths kicking a soccer ball around, old people gathering for the daily soup kitchen, some working in a freshly planted vegetable garden. There are well-tended flowerbeds, neat lawns and simple, breeze-block build-ings, more open space than you can find elsewhere in Diepsloot.

The MaTikkun centre is run by Donald Nghonyama, a busi-nesslike man who sits in a simple, sparsely decorated office. Donald had a long history of working in development, particu-larly with youth, before being recruited by Tikkun to fix up this centre. He tells his story in detail and with a strong sense of pride in what he has achieved.

Born and schooled in Limpopo, he wanted to be a doctor, but 'my matric results and family situation were not supportive enough'. He studied teaching at the Johannesburg College of Education, 'though I had no intention of being a teacher'. He got a job at a private school.

He volunteered at the Anglican Church's Thumalong Mission and became the co-ordinator of the centre, which included a school, a community clinic, a nutrition centre and an early child-hood development centre. He was acting principal of the school for a year, and then deputy principal. 'I moved from there to work with people with disabilities, heading the disability pro-gramme. The centre was near Klipgat, by the Morula Sun, and we also started a centre in Hammanskraal.'

The centre was getting broken into every weekend, and this got him thinking about dealing with youth and crime. 'It was young people causing this problem in Winterveldt and I felt we had to do something about it. So I researched a project to work with young people involved in crime.

'I discovered this model called Make a Difference, and was

impressed with it. When Mandela released young people from prison, I was asked to lead the initiative. There was only one Life Centre, a pilot programme in the Eastern Cape, so I went to see it, came back and started my leadership centre in Winterveldt called Bokanosa (Future).

'It did wonders that centre, working with many young people, some known to be hard-core criminals in the community who had been arrested and re-arrested. I have many stories to tell from that centre about how youth changed.'

The Dutch Embassy selected him as one of ten people to go to Holland and look at programmes for young people at risk. On his return, he decided to go back to his home province of Limpopo and work with youth there. 'It was different there. There was not so much a problem of crime, but a problem of poverty and of young people being left by parents who went to work far away.'

He started a new organisation which grew to 12 centres around the province and 180 staff over the next seven years. He still sits on the board, but went from there to work with the National Youth Development Agency to repeat the Bokanosa model in Eersterus, near Pretoria. Sixteen months later, he was recruited by MaTikkun. 'The centre was here, but there were problems with projects and some were not running. We have managed now, a year later, to stabilise the organisation, it is now running as expected, and there is room for growth.'

He calls the model they are using at the MaTikkun Centre a Circle of Care – a combination of home-based care for those who need it, family support, an early child development programme, a youth development programme and a feeding scheme. Their team of nine home-based carers do the fieldwork and identify the sick and needy, an assessment is done and if there are young children then social workers are brought in. They first attend to the needs of the youngest, and have a good relationship with the school on the same premises where they can be placed. Or they might be put in the early childhood development centre. If they have no clothes, they'll find a sponsor, if their shack is falling apart they'll find someone to fix it. 'We do this for the children in the family,' he says. If necessary, once a month they will get a food and care pack (sugar, mealie meal, rice, washing powder and vaseline); there is lunch at the centre every weekday, and a bakkie goes around every day delivering food to those who cannot get there. The youth development programme has a computer centre, library, a learning support programme and an indoor sports area, which is also used for arts and culture. 'We are finding children in grades 5/6/7 who can't read or write, and they benefit from this programme.'

He has a staff of 65, about 45 of whom are former beneficiaries or their families. 'So we ensure that there is skill in the family that will bring income. They are trained in home-based care, or gardening, or cooking … and then they are employed.' The annual budget for this centre is about R5-million, which comes from the national lottery and corporate donors.

When Donald was in Mpumalanga, he joined political organisations. Here, he has to work with them but has little time for them. 'There are no leaders I respect in Diepsloot because most seem to have their own agenda. There are stories [of corruption] linked to many of them.'

I go out for a day with the caregivers on their walk-around, which takes me into the most ramshackle households of all: those unable to care for themselves, most with HIV/Aids and entirely dependent on the food parcels and extraordinary support of the caregivers.

The nine caregivers look after about 125 households, but have only enough food parcels for 75 of them. The rest are on waiting lists. Some of them are standard RDP houses, reasonably comfortable but with elderly or sickly residents who need help; most are precarious, windswept hellholes whose inhabitants have barely enough food or warmth to sustain themselves.

The caregivers wash the sick, find a blanket if someone doesn't have one, give food when they can, teach them about hygiene, clean the place if it needs it and make sure they take their medication. Sometimes they take them to the clinic. Sometimes they just check them out, offer a sympathetic ear and some advice.

The caregivers walk many miles every day since they do not have a vehicle, dealing with people in the most dire and depressing circumstances. One man we visit is having trouble sealing his rickety shack against rain, cold and rats, which he laughingly says run over him during the night. He is using plastic and newspaper to try and cover the gaps between the walls and the roof, or to seal off holes. On his wall is a sign: 'Just don't forget who's boss!'

Another expresses gratitude to the caregivers for having found him a blanket – he was previously sleeping under plastic. The caregivers congratulate one old man for keeping the place in order, saying last time they were there, the place was in a very bad state and they had to sweep and scrub it. From the smell of fire and the metal container in the room, it is clear he does not have paraffin and is having to light a fire to cook and warm the room. Another old lady lives in a house packed with furniture, so that one can barely move in it. The television is playing quietly in a corner. They visit her to help her because she has had a hip operation, can no longer work and sometimes needs help doing things. She is on a pension, but it only covers her food. She tells me she came from Zevenfontein back in 1994, and now has an RDP house. On the other hand, Anna lives in a tiny shack, and there is nowhere to sit. I am offered the only chair and others sit on the dusty, uncovered floor. Anna is young and looking after an old lady, sitting on the bed, in the most bedraggled clothes.

A woman who will only give me her initials, BN, makes her living looking after kids during the day in a private crèche. Five kids are sleeping on the floor. While we are there, a mother rushing off to work drops off a kid, with a packet of nappies, a bottle and a blanket. BN tells the caregivers she is no longer vomiting, but has pains in 'the back of my shoulders'. She was working as a domestic and came to Diepsloot 10 years ago for a place to live 'when that job finished'. She is due a pension, she says, but can't access it because she has no ID. The caregivers hand her a food parcel and help her take her medicine. They are picking up those on the bottom of the pile who can't access state assistance.

After many hours of walking, a weary caregiver says: 'There are too many challenges, just too many challenges.' They really need a vehicle to get around the place better and be able to visit more people each day. 'We have to have so much patience in Diepsloot. MaTikkun is trying, but the people are too much and the needs are high.'

The Three Ladies of Lonehill were members of a small suburban church who had come together to do something about the pre-schools of Diepsloot. They formed a formidable team: Patti, who used her substantial public relations contacts in the corporate world to raise money, Anne, a missionary who had worked for 35 years in pre-schools, and Milly Jarvis, the cook.

I meet Patti Henley at the Mugg & Bean coffee shop in Lonehill Centre. 'You won't miss me. I wear a large white hat,' she said. She certainly did.

Patti had been in marketing for years, running her own events management business, and had been involved in the high-profile Presidential Golf Day. She used to volunteer to teach at the Riversands school, just outside Diepsloot: 'We noticed there were no pre-schools in Diepsloot at all, and there were about 100 kids at Riversands who had no pre-schooling and had never been taught fine-motor skills or stuff like that. They could not use a pair of scissors.

'One morning at a meeting at our church, the ladies said

they wanted to do something and someone said we should do a pre-school. My heart went duff-duff,' she says, thumping her chest with a fist, 'duff-duff, because I knew it was exactly what I wanted to do.'

The farmer at Riversands gave them a corner of his land to use, and three of the church ladies started with just 11 kids. Patti approached her public relations clients, like Nedbank and Investec, and they helped her start the pre-school in February 1993, alongside an existing primary school. In March that year they had their first annual fundraising golf day, and 'in no time the school was bursting with kids'.

For 17 years they struggled to register the school, with red tape all the way and a long list of technical requirements to meet – from the kind of paint they used on the walls, to an ex-traction fan over the stove. When I met Patti in 2010, they were now registered, but still struggling to get state support for either an extra teacher or their feeding scheme.

After a while, Patti changed to a new church in Rivonia where they were less interested in the pre-school and wanted to run a feeding scheme. The pre-school now had 70 kids but the primary school had over 1 000 and kids were coming to class hungry. Patti helped raise money and they now feed over 1 000 children three times a week. They have set up gardens to grow vegetables and their sponsors sometimes come and help them cook and serve.

Esther Phiri had started as cook and cleaner at the pre-school, but in time had taken over teaching one of the classes. Then she had said she would go and start her own school in Diepsloot – and it now had 55 kids. Patti had raised money to build a class-room on to Esther's house and fix a leaking roof.

Four years ago, a missionary named Anne Theunissen who had been a pre-school teacher for 35 years joined Patti's church. 'She got involved in Riversands and said we could do a lot bet-ter. She said we could develop proper teaching structures and curricula.' Anne drew up a plan for Riversands, and then some of the other pre-schools which had popped up in Diepsloot, and now they were providing curricula for a network of about 20 schools with over 1 000 children spread through the settlement. 'Ninety per cent of my time is now in Diepsloot. I gave up all other projects at the beginning of this year, and kept just a few clients to pay the bills,' Patti said.

Now they had their threesome: Patti raised the money, Anne did the teaching and curriculum, Milly ran the feeding scheme.

The next phase came when they realised that some of these kids had never received a Christmas present. They held a special November golf day and every kid in the system now gets one – and it has become an annual event.

Perhaps Patti's most unlikely triumph was fixing one of Diepsloot's worst roads. 'It was a road I used to use every week to go to one of the pre-schools, but it was so bad that it would take me about 20 minutes just on that one road. I had talked before to the MD of WBH [a large construction company] and he had told me to come back the following year. I was driving to Diepsloot one day and saw their trucks fixing a nearby road, so I wrote to him again. He wrote back quickly and said he would do something.

'He sent an engineer who said it was not just a case of grading the road, they had to shore up the sides. But it could be done and it so happened his team in the area had three free days coming up.

'I had to get permission. I made an appointment with a guy from the street committee, he sent me to the councillor, who said it needed to go to the Joburg Roads Agency, so that was a third meeting. To cover my arse I wrote a letter to them …

'WBH wanted some mileage from it, so I organised press and television, but everyone was busy because of the World Cup. I fought with [nearby suburban newspaper] *Fourways Review* because they said they could not do a story in Diepsloot. On the third day, all the directors came, the councillors came and we had a ribbon cutting. The kids from the pre-school came with big paper hands they had made and did a thank you.

'Then a man came and confronted me. He said he was from the ANC and was on the street committee, and we didn't have his permission. He insisted that we do his road as well.'

The missionary Patti talked to me about, Anne Theunissen, took me on her weekly round of the pre-schools. I arranged to meet them at the Riversands school and she arrived in a kombi with her husband, daughter, grandson and dog, all of whom had piled in to come all the way from Alberton to help. Her husband, a school teacher, had arranged to take every Wednesday off to do this, and his role was to compile the list of kids for the Christmas presents. The daughter did the financials, collecting R10 a month for each copy of the worksheets her mother prepared. And Anne prepared these worksheets and guided the teachers in how to use them.

Four years ago, Anne and her husband had sold up everything and were on their way to Namibia, where she had been asked to write a pre-school programme. But she was refused a visa and could not stay. On that trip, one night she had 'a terrible dream with a newborn baby that sat up and looked at me and I knew I had to look after and care for that baby'. It haunted her for a long time. When she joined the new church and they asked her to get involved in their pre-school scheme, her husband said: 'This is it. This is your dream. Go and do it!'

She had the curriculum she had written for Namibia, and wanted to try it out. 'There are lots of pre-school learning programmes out there, but none of them are very African,' she said.

A few years on, and 'I have found peace with this work,' she said. 'I have grown to love this place very much. Now I know what that dream was about.'

At one stage they had 23 schools in the scheme. 'Some were

very good and used the worksheets properly, others just handed it out to the kids.' In one school we visit, Anne finds the teacher taking children through a worksheet dealing with the senses of sweet and sour, chanting the words. 'But you can't teach it without giving them something sweet and something sour,' she says irritably. 'Then it is just rote learning.'

Anne insists that each parent contribute R10 to the worksheets. 'I have to get back some costs, and parents have to take charge of this. I can't give it free to some schools and not others.' It is late in the year and at this time, she says, many parents stop paying, or the teachers collect the R10 and spend it before it gets to Anne, and so she has to cut them off. Her list of participating schools is down to 18 now, 'and dropping'.

'I get despondent,' she says, 'but I just plod on. This time of year, it can be very disheartening, but I just plod on.'

One day she was driving past a taxi rank in her kombi and the taxi-drivers, suspecting her of poaching on their territory, had aggressively boxed her in, surrounded her and got out of their cars threateningly. 'I just smiled and waved and one person recognised me. He gestured everyone away, took my hand and kissed it. "We know what you do for us," he said.'

Riversands is a picturesque little school, done in Bryanston style, neat and well-kept with a well-equipped playground. But it is just outside Diepsloot, so transport is a difficulty for many parents. The schools I see in Diepsloot range enormously, from some that are quite decent, with neat rows of bags and equipment, and teachers engaged with a cheerful bunch of children. All of them are crowded. But some are packed into dark rooms, with children clearly left to do their own thing, and very rough toilet and kitchen facilities. One has a bucket in a corner of the plot for a toilet, others have broken windows and leaking roofs ...

Patti is working hard at bringing corporate sponsors to see, so they will get involved and fix up these schools. Anne is training teachers, to try and get them to a Level 5 certification, which will enable them to access state subsidies. Milly is feeding and feeding …

I stumble across two contrasting examples of corporate social involvement in Diepsloot. One day, driving towards the place, two large luxury buses are on the road. They turn off into Diepsloot, stop outside the Lesedi Centre for the Disabled, and disgorge what look like well-heeled tourists. I pass by a while later and am surprised to see lots of people hard at work, painting, hammering, planting, fixing, a hive of activity with their sleeves rolled up, some with clipboards supervising and guiding, all of it systematic and organised. It is the office staff of Internet Solutions, one of the country's major internet providers, out for a day of social involvement and participation. When they leave, the place is shining with a new coat of paint, the gardens have been planted, buildings fixed, it all looks spick and span, and there is a big sign identifying Internet Solutions as the sponsor.

Late in 2010, management from Montecasino, the giant luxury casino a few kilometres away, were found in an unlikely huddle in an unlikely place, meeting with the ANC Youth League in the Diepsloot Kentucky Fried Chicken outlet. This is the culmination of a long Youth League battle to engage the nearby casino and divert some of its resources Diepsloot's way.

Youth League leader Phillip Makwela had approached the casino about a year previously to ask them about their relationship to Diepsloot. 'At first, they sent me from pillar to post, from office to office, until I threatened to expose them. I told them the Youth League would mobilise the people from Diepsloot to march to their premises to inquire about the conditions in which Montecasino got their licence.' The Youth Leaguers knew that casinos had promised large-scale social involvement in surrounding communities when they applied for licences, and they wanted to make sure some of this came to their constituency.

The threat worked. 'Out of the blue, I received a phone call from Sizwe Jantjies, who spoke to me for more than two hours. He tried to explain that Montecasino does not account to the Youth League.' But Phillip extracted a promise that they would provide a copy of their licence agreement and a list of corporate social investment projects. A month went by with nothing, and then Jantjies called to ask for a meeting.

At the KFC meeting, Jantjies said they were ready to come and engage. They planned and called a wider meeting and established a joint committee that would meet regularly. This committee held its first meeting in January 2011, this time in a more formal setting at the nearby Indaba Hotel. Montecasino management laid out a long-term agenda: they were to work as one committee, one team of equals to seek interventions to improve conditions in Diepsloot and bring to bear Montecasino's power and resources. They elected a local pastor as convenor of the joint committee and agreed to meet monthly.

This is a 10 or 20-year project. 'Montecasino is the leading business in the area, and we have a responsibility to develop this area,' they said.

I find no end of NGOs active in one way or another in Diepsloot, in all sorts of ways. They are an integral part of the small, incipient local economy. They pick up some of those who have fallen through the state's welfare net, but they also introduce skills, organisation and some resources on top of those resources brought in by those who have employment, by government projects and grants.

In the local suburban media, I read about the Akani Foundation, whose after-school care for about 450 kids was featured when a casino donated four yellowwood trees for their garden. A media release alerted me to a large-scale youth festival organised by Diepsloot Youth Projects, which undertakes a number of activities for youth.

Global Studio – which was involved in the creation of Diepsloot's Arts and Culture Network – brings architecture, urban planning and engineering students from around the world together for two weeks to tackle issues in places like Diepsloot. They sent me an e-mail invitation to a publicity event. 'Wassup!' it says, with a picture of a Diepsloot shared toilet. 'Imagine your home, full of people and family, life, music, laughter, the way we all wish our homes to be, but then you feel the call of nature,' it reads. 'You step out of your house, onto a dirty street, wait in a queue, jump the puddle to get into the toilet cubicle, and nearly slip for the mould gathering from so much toilet leakage, try to shut the door but one hinge is broken so you have to lift it into place, there's a hole as large as your head so people can see in, there is no seat.' They had developed a way to improve and repair the drains, but had no more funding. Now they were having a promotional day where kids were painting the toilets and they were hoping to raise funds.

The local branch of Global Voices is run by an energetic and determined Australian, Jennifer van den Bussche, who I ran into all over the place in Diepsloot. The volunteer students were grappling with things like how to keep the toilets working and how to insulate shacks – issues of basic maintenance, fundamental to living conditions, which the authorities would pay no attention to when their policy was to remove these settlements – and Van den Bussche could often be found organising to get toilets repaired, helping mobilise a community radio station, shrugging her shoulders at the authorities, smiling wryly at it all.

An NGO with a markedly different approach and a distinctive community-building strategy is the Seriti Institute, led by Gavin Andersson, a tall and well-built figure with a gentle demeanour. He was a trade unionist back in the 1970s and 1980s, before being banned, forced into exile and settling in Botswana for some years where he worked and studied development.

His approach grows out of the PhD he did, bringing together his politics, his history of collective action and a passion for community work built around the thinking of South American writer Paulo Freire. He is the driving force behind Seriti, and has surrounded himself with a high-powered team of professionals and activists. They work out of a suburban house, but have a rigour and organisation that feels more corporate than non-profit.

Seriti ended up in Diepsloot in error: they were meant to be in Vlakfontein, developing and training for a community work programme, but the city councillors there could not agree where they should be based. The city suggested Diepsloot as the alternative.

'The thinking behind what we do is that this country has all the resources to thrive – we have the funds and we have the smarts. What's missing is an ability to organise for development,' Andersson says. Seriti scopes an area like Diepsloot, identifies the main challenges and some specific projects to tackle and finds about 250 volunteers. They purchase what they need to do these projects – absolutely everything, from cars to coffee cups. Then they call together the volunteers, tell them to form themselves into an organisation to undertake these tasks, and quote to do them. They are loaned the equipment for one month, and told that they will have to pay for anything – even a teaspoon – which is not returned. The volunteers say what they can do, at what price, and in what time frame, and if their bid is competitive, Seriti pays them to do it. There could not be a more marked difference to the hand-out approach of most NGOs.

While the work is being done, Seriti runs an Organisational Workshop, teaching the participants the theory and practice of organising themselves. During the month, they invariably restructure their organisation. At the end of the month, Seriti takes their equipment and leaves, and what remains is a structure, usually tied to an official community work programme –

a government job-creation programme which pays the unemployed two days a week to do community work. Seriti teaches them 'to assess what is needed to complete each project, negotiate contracts and manage people up to the completion of each project'.

In Diepsloot, the participants renovated a school, including building toilets and electrifying the classrooms, resurrected a failing agricultural project, ran a campaign against alcohol abuse, fixed up a taxi rank, promoted HIV education, cleared a dangerous river crossing, trained 10 school sports coaches, provided early childhood development skills to teachers in 18 crèches. At the end of the month, they had formed Thusanang Diepsloot, with a constitution and bank account, and had completed many of the tasks. Perhaps the biggest triumph was the agricultural project, which had been selling only about R1 000 worth of goods a month, and now sells R120 000 and employs 18 people. But in their report at the end of the month, the Seriti organisers were more interested in how the participants had organised themselves. At the beginning, they had formed a simple top-down structure and called in the local councillor to help run meetings. By the end, they had a participatory co-ordinating committee and – according to Seriti – had taken on board the lesson that they had to manage themselves and not take direction from outside.

'One of the big issues is always dealing with the existing organisational elite,' Andersson says. 'The extent to which you go along with this structure is the extent to which you can be successful.' In Diepsloot, the problem was a city councillor seeking to influence things from the sideline, and his cronies sitting up all night to caucus what to do in the project. The Seriti people had to intervene to tell the politicians that they would do better to let things happen and not try to control it.

'I learnt that it is not easy,' writes Moses Kobe, who was elected chair of Thusanang, in his report. 'However, we were able to finish some of the work allocated to us. We are grateful to the Seriti people for teaching us how to run an organisation. As the chairperson, I have also learnt a lot about running an organisation in a sustainable way, long after the Seriti people have left.

'Together we can do more,' he concludes.

Seriti works with over 70 000 people in about 70 locations. Their goals are large: to have mobilised 270 000 people by 2014, working with the government's community work programme.

In Diepsloot, they were surprised by the low level of skill and knowledge. 'We work in all sorts of communities, and always there are geniuses who emerge, people who can just get things done.

'Here, people had no general knowledge and no history. They could not say what happened in April 1994 (when South African held its first democratic elections). They did not understand the work process or how value was created. This meant there was extreme individualism – with people just wanting to hustle something for themselves – and sometimes a mob response, reacting with aggression as a group when there was a difficulty'; also what they called 'immediatism' – the tendency to do something with immediate benefit – like help oneself to T-shirts – without thinking of the consequences.

CHAPTER ELEVEN

Off the record

To make it into the media if you are from Diepsloot, you have to be either seriously evil or lucky enough to be touched by those really good; there's little of interest in between.

The evil who make it into media are those who kill or destroy in acts of crime. There are those who kill or destroy in a greyer moral area, such as crime prevention or political protest. Either of these modes will get you into the media, but a combination guarantees the widest coverage.

What you get into depends on who your victim is. Murder within Diepsloot will get you the *Daily Sun*, but not the broadsheets; you have to kill someone from outside Diepsloot or destroy state property in the course of a protest to make the more serious newspapers.

Alternatively, you can be touched by the forces of good. People from outside doing good works in the area have a fair chance of making the local media: a casino planting trees, a feisty woman pulling strings to have a street graded, or a famous tennis player adopting a youth project. And, of course, a charismatic politician dropping in for tea. These acts are sometimes done for the purposes of media coverage, and done by those who know how to get exposure, so you can usually rely on it.

If you are a Diepslooter, don't expect to be quoted in most

newspapers: very few voices from Diepsloot are heard, other than those of officials or crime survivors. The notable exception is the *Daily Sun*, which specialises in using the voices of ordinary people and seldom quotes those of politicians and experts.

I study 18 months of coverage of Diepsloot in all the newspapers, local and national. Diepsloot appears in the press in spates when there is a violent incident, or when a national politician pays it some attention. The mayor or a provincial MEC does not quite crack it. Of 244 mentions I find in the newspapers in this time, 56 per cent are crime reports, 12 per cent deal with residents protesting, 7 per cent report the visit of a cabinet minister, MP or mayor; and only about 6 per cent offer stories about the way people live in the area.

Of course, this tells us more about the South African media than it does about Diepsloot. Of the 28 human interest stories, every single one of them is in one newspaper, the *Daily Sun*, a relatively new working class tabloid that is the paper most likely to be read by the people of Diepsloot, and it features stories like the 48-year-old virgin in search of a husband (and the triumphant follow-up when the newspaper helped her find one), or children or the elderly who have gone missing – a hardy perennial. The *Daily Sun's* coverage is overwhelmingly about crime, with barely a mention of protests or politicians; the other newspapers tell us only about protests and politicians, and barely mention crime unless it is aimed at those driving past on the road. But the people of Diepsloot find themselves in the *Daily Sun*; for the rest of the media, they are the inhabitants of a strange, distant and somewhat threatening land.

The *Daily Sun* features the more bizarre stories of daily life in Diepsloot and shows some quite important social trends that readers of the other newspapers may be oblivious to. Most of their coverage is of crime (70 per cent), which often makes the front page if there are bloody and gruesome pictures to go with it, and mob justice features in at least one story a week. If you read the *Daily Sun*, you can see that mob justice is a growing problem, but you might miss this in most of the other newspapers, which cover it only occasionally. Most of the rest of the *Daily Sun*'s stories fall into the category of human interest (20 per cent). In fact, the *Daily Sun* relies almost entirely on ordinary people as sources, using police when there is a crime, but entirely ignoring the antics of politicians, either local or national. You will see an official quoted if it is a matter in the hands of courts or police, but not otherwise. And you will never see the words of an expert commentator.

The difference, of course, is that the *Daily Sun* is the only paper that takes the people of Diepsloot seriously as readers, and not merely subjects of distant interest when something happens that might impact on the outside world. Being an archetypal populist tabloid, it is focused on researching and delivering exactly what those readers want from a daily paper, and as closely as possible referencing their lives, their concerns and their needs. If people in Diepsloot are xenophobic, this is reflected in the *Daily Sun*. It was the only paper to cover growing incidents of xenophobia before early 2009, though it was slow to cover the big outburst – possibly because it was less unusual or unexpected to them – but then did it with a relish that caused some controversy. A front-page editorial appeared to justify the xenophobia, agreeing that foreigners were taking jobs and houses from locals; the paper spoke out more firmly against the violence a few weeks later.

The *Daily Sun* is the only daily paper with serious circulation in the area. Since the conventional newspaper distribution network does not reach into areas such as Diepsloot, they contract a resident as their agent. He sells about 4 000 *Daily Sun* copies daily, and about 500 copies of *City Press* on a Sunday. Since he makes about R1 a copy (some of which he has to share with a sub-contractor), he is a thriving local entrepreneur. But he is being contained. He told me that he had expanded his newspaper distribution into another settlement, not far away, and had been thriving there. The *Daily Sun* gave that franchise to someone else, and made him stick to Diepsloot.

Other papers tend to parachute their reporters in on special occasions, and this often means that reporters have no sense of the differences, disputes and tensions that lie behind what they witness, who they quote and why things are being said. So a year after the visit of Minister Tokyo Sexwale, a newspaper interviews someone about it – but with no apparent knowledge that this person is from a faction that felt excluded from the visit, did not like the way it was organised, and seeks an opportunity to denounce the Minister. This is not to say the view is not valid, just difficult to understand and explain fully if you don't know that background. What you end up with is the cheap-shot story: Tokyo's visit meant nothing to us ...

That is the main reason Diepslooters are so contemptuous of the media as a whole, and so quick to say that they only give a bad side to their story.

The most cavernous gap, though, is the lack of coverage from the public broadcaster. You would expect the SABC with its public service obligations to give voice to the people of Diepsloot and treat them seriously as both subjects and audience. Lack of attention from commercial media, for whom this is not their audience, is understandable – even if their audience needs to know more about places like Diepsloot. But it is hard to understand why there is not fuller coverage of these places in the medium which is supposed to do what is not financially viable for the commercial media.

I spend a day chasing dead bodies with the *Daily Sun's* Diepsloot reporter, Kola Alli, and freelance photographer Golden Mtika. 'Come on the weekend,' Kola says to me. 'That's when people are drunk and stuff happens.'

Saturday starts at the new police satellite station, where Kola is clearly at home. All the policemen know him and are quick to tell him what happened during the night, but they are nervous of my presence and make it clear that none of their names are to appear. 'If you want comment, you will have to go to the colonel. We will get into a lot of trouble if our names are there,' a constable says to me. It was a routine Friday night. 'We didn't sleep,' a detective says, 'I was called out to two murders during the night. Actually one murder with house robbery and one attempted murder, but the woman was shot in the head, so I don't think she will survive.'

Kola hangs around for half an hour to pick up stories, getting names and addresses, talking to the dozen or so people milling around at any time to find out what they are reporting or complaining about. The satellite station is new, fresh and neat. Kola is wandering in and out of the charge room and other offices.

There is no holding cell, but a woman is waiting in the back of a patrol van to be taken to the Erasmia station. Kola finds out that she has been accused of stealing some clothes – not a very exciting story. But another young woman, looking dishevelled, says her boyfriend burnt down her shack after an argument the previous night. She knows where he is and some policemen jump in a vehicle to go and arrest him. Kola takes her story down and makes a note to follow up later with the police.

'I make sure I am friendly with all the policemen,' Kola says. 'That is where I get my stories, and I need them to fill me in on what has happened.'

Kola is slim and casually dressed, in white jeans and a bright green golf-shirt, clutching an open notebook all the time. 'I want to build my career as a crime reporter,' he says. Kola lives in Pretoria and comes to Diepsloot, where he has carved out a beat for himself, in his battered old car which he has to manoeuvre very slowly through Diepsloot's rocky roads.

Golden is suave and muscular with a carefully shaped little beard, always carrying a backpack with his camera discreetly inside. He lives in Diepsloot. Recently his equipment was stolen and he was unable to work for some time before he could replace it.

'It is very tough to live here – there is too much crime. Every month-end we chase more than 10 murders. And because of this, mob justice becomes the order of the day. They suspect someone of a crime, the community comes together and go after him,' he says. 'They beat him with hammers, golf sticks, sharp objects, there is even necklacing. They don't trust the police, and there is ignorance of the law. They see someone get bail and they think they are free and not punished. So they get aggressive.'

Golden's scoop was to capture on video recently the full process of a captured criminal being chased, beaten, publicly humiliated, and then burnt alive. The BBC bought the material and are now offering him six months of training as a cameraman, he says. But he is sick of gory pictures and dead bodies. 'People used to call me at three in the morning to tell me something is happening, there was a shooting or a stabbing, but I don't take those calls any more,' he says. 'I have had enough.'

Foreign correspondents regularly use these two as stringers when they need a quick fix on poverty, crime and mob justice. Parachute in, and these guys are there to guide you. Their perspective, though, is singularly around crime and mob justice.

We walk down the road to the murder scene, and all along the way people are greeting and chatting to Kola and Golden. The streets are lively on a Saturday morning, with a cacophony of competing noises – music blaring out of shops, builders banging and sawing, cars hooting, some of the taverns already full and rowdy. It is a hot summer's day, but it has been raining, so the streets are muddy, there are pools of water everywhere and the sewage is flowing.

In Atlantic Street, where the murder of Tsepo Masedi took place, Kola and Golden ask around and find the deceased's best friend. But he is in no mood to talk, just bowing his head and turning away. We are pointed to the brother of the deceased, who shows us the crime scene. Tsepo was in bed with his girlfriend when four men started breaking down the door. The girlfriend hid under the blankets, but Tsepo tried to stop them entering. They shot him, found his and her cellphones and R20 cash, and left quickly. What the brother can't understand is why they came straight to the shack, as if they were targeting Tsepo specifically.

A small crowd gathers to listen to the story, and there is a great deal of nodding when Golden says, 'For R20, they kill someone. For just R20. They use the same gun to rob a bank and to steal a cellphone.'

We find the girlfriend, Niniwe Moilwe, a few blocks away in a backyard shack of an RDP house. She is miserable, but willing to talk when she hears it is the *Daily Sun*. She says they threatened to rape her and shot her boyfriend when he protested, before fleeing. She had made sure she did not see any faces, as she would then have been shot too. Golden snaps a picture while Kola interviews her.

From there it is back to the police station. Kola and Golden do this every Friday, Saturday and Sunday, picking up the crop of stories to feed the *Daily Sun*. With at least two murders every weekend, you need a twist in the tale to get them into the paper. This one makes the front page with the headline 'Shoot me!: Niniwe's lover chose death to protect her!'

'Niniwe Moilwe (30) has learned a tragic lesson in the power of love.

Her brave boyfriend pleaded with thugs: 'Don't make me watch while you rape her … leave her alone … rather shoot me instead!'

Tsepo Masedi (34) paid the highest price to protect the woman he loved. It cost him his life! It happened in the dark hours of Saturday morning at Diepsloot, north of Joburg'.

It seems to me that Niniwe may have been struck by the power of hate and guns, rather than of love. But who is to argue when the *Daily Sun* has the dead man's quotes.

That is the outside media. Most notable, though, is the absence of local or community outlets in which politicians could communicate and the public respond, needs and aspirations could be expressed, debates held and the voices of Diepsloot heard and fed into the outside media. There has been no such media, and it has a profound impact on the politics and development of the place.

For one thing, the lack of community media means that rumours abound and infest the political sphere. The 2010 protests broke out because people believed a story that they were being moved to Brits. Claims about rival politicians race around, with loose, untested allegations being made by all of them against all the others. Allegations of corruption fester and pollute the atmosphere with little mechanism for such stories to be tested and, if true, pursued. In a volatile situation, a rumour can put a match to the kindling.

It also means that the authorities and politicians are not held to their promises in the way they might be if they were reported in local media. When the building work on the police station stops, people talk and speculate on the cause but have to wait for officials to call a consultation meeting, at their convenience and with their invited guests, to explain the problem. The officials and politicians I speak to all give different timetables for the plan to build another batch of houses in the area – and none of them bear any relation to reality. It is as if you can say what you like, since it is seldom recorded in public in a way that you might have to account for.

Good journalists are those trained to ask the right questions and push for answers, and know when they are getting the runaround. At consultative meetings, not many people are emboldened to speak, or equipped to challenge those in authority. A local journalist would have the licence to do it. And the absence of such a person is noticeable at all these meetings, which go unreported and unrecorded.

Above all, the absence of media means that if people have something to say, or demand, or reject, or argue, or pursue, or campaign for or against, they can either wait for election time, or they can go to a public consultation meeting, or they can take to the streets in protest. The absence of media means there are fewer legitimate channels for the expression of views outside of public protest which so often turns to violence. The absence of media is one of the most disempowering elements of life in Diepsloot. People are only victims and subjects of media, and can seldom make or shape news, or pursue their interests via the media, short of taking to the streets.

In the wealthier suburbs, potholes or street lights which don't work make it into the newspaper and radio stations, often with outrage at the deterioration of standards. There is almost no coverage of the fact that Diepsloot's roads are in such a shocking state that a 4x4 has trouble negotiating many of them. Diepsloot's residents can only get their roads, or lack of street lights, or other service issues, into the media by taking to the streets and making a noise, perhaps causing violence. Then they are noticed.

In January 2011, I get an email from a Diepsloot contact in Diepsloot. 'You may have heard what happened last night. A gang of thugs went on the rampage and killed seven people ... some of them were apprehended and killed by a mob of angry community members.' The gang was made up of 17 thugs he told me.

This happens on a Friday night. On Saturday and Sunday I watch television, listen to radio, scan the papers, and there is not a mention. I hear that the MEC for Safety and Security is coming to be briefed by community leaders and I think that will bring media attention. But still nothing. On Monday, the *Daily Sun* duly reports that it was actually two people who were murdered, a husband and wife, but their main angle is the murder of the murderers. 'Fiery justice … in the town that takes no prisoners', is the headline. There is nothing in the other media.

Four days after the incident, *The Star* gets interested when a protest breaks out. 'Enraged residents threatened to storm and burn the local police station after seven alleged perpetrators of mob justice were arrested last night.' The story now is the protest and the murder of 'three people killed in the latest incidents of mob justice', with barely a mention of the origins of the incident. The problem, they say, is that 'a mob claiming to represent residents fed up with crime are waging a reign of terror in the township'. So it was not the gang who were responsible for the 'terror', it was the crowd that reacted when police did not arrive. The original murder is mentioned in the last paragraph of a long story. In the second paragraph is the murder of the murderers. 'It's all organised crime,' they quote someone saying – talking about the crowd that committed the street justice, not those who carried out the original killing. This all compounds confusion around an area like Diepsloot, a sense that it is a place of random and irrational mob violence, and contributes to people's bewilderment and fear. It is a perfect example of the effects of rumour: numbers escalated as the story spread.

I learn later from a foreign correspondent who investigated this particular incident that the two alleged gang members who were caught and killed by the crowd died in quite separate incidents, hours apart. One in fact was set on fire after he was dead and not while in a shack. Nor was there any sign that these two were a part of the 'mythical 17' who were blamed for the first attack which sparked the reaction. In fact, one appears to be a tragic case of wrong identification. But in Diepsloot, and in the media reports, there is just a cloud of dangerous myths and rumours, and exaggerated numbers.

There are two current attempts to introduce local media in Diepsloot. A small group of volunteers have been pushing to start a community radio station for two to three years. Their progress has been painfully slow, mainly because they are short of the resources and skills to make it happen. To do so, they have to put together a difficult technical application to the regulator for a low-power licence; they have to do a business plan for the Media Development and Democracy Agency, the state agency which assists such stations; they have to apply to the Department of Communications for assistance in equipping and building a studio, they have to form a trust and register it with the High Court, and they have to find training for the skills needed to set up and run a station. In all of this, they will have to show they have a viable business plan and a reasonable chance of success at getting enough funding or advertising to stay afloat. This is no easy task – and I am drafted into helping them; they will probably get on the air in the next year or two.

An attempt at a local newspaper was carried out by two energetic and impressive young entrepreneurs, one a university student. It was called *Loxion Connect* and lasted a few editions before being bought out by Lucky Moshimane, Diepsloot's millionaire businessman, who used it as a base for a larger paper, the *Noweto News*. This tabloid was launched in October 2010, with a strong ANC presence, Moshimane being a key sponsor and supporter of the party.

At the launch, ANC branch chair Chris Vondo said he hoped 'this newspaper will become the voice of the poor in the northern suburbs. ... This paper will enable communities to tell our own stories and will serve again as an educational tool.' He set out a dual, contradictory role for the paper – independent of corrupt leaders, but close to government. '*Noweto News* must not become the mouthpiece of corrupt leaders. If one leader is corrupt, this newspaper must be able to publish the news without fear or favour. At the same time, it must work together with government to further assist in issues of development.' And to this onerous task, he added a commercial role: 'We believe this newspaper will provide a platform to small businesses to expose them to other markets so that their produce and products are sold.'

The other branch chair, Rogers Makhubele, focused on trying to change Diepsloot's image: 'We challenge this paper to highlight the beauty of our community as opposed to other publications that always project a negative image of our township.' But he too wanted it to be close to government: 'We plead with the team again to get inputs from the senior leadership in government with regards to issues of development.'

As it happens, the first edition of the paper appeared to be little more than a publicity outlet for its patron, Lucky Moshimane. There are photos of him on five of the eight pages – all but the classified adverts, the sports page and the 'Noweto babes' picture spread.

Another attempt to talk to the outside world is the diepsloot. com website, which provided my initial entry-point into the area. 'After the 2008 xenophobic violence,' says Phillip Makwela, one of those who put it together, 'we browsed the web searching for stuff about Diepsloot and we found nothing, only government stuff about projects here. The only coverage of this area was when there was the violence. Otherwise there was nothing.'

'We want the people of Diepsloot to tell their own stories – good and bad.'

Lessons from Bullfrogs

When Jacob Zuma won the ANC presidency in 2007, I wrote a newspaper column asking why the media had called it so wrong, why we journalists were apparently so out of touch with sentiment in the country. It was, I said, because our eyes were cast upwards rather than downwards. We were watching the corridors of power – Parliament, the Union Buildings and Luthuli House – rather than what was happening on the ground in the townships, the informal settlements and the local ANC branches. There was too much political speculation and too little of the reportage that would have told us more of what ANC membership and leadership were saying and what was driving change in the ANC.

This perspective has characterised much of my journalism career. I was part of the group which had launched a newspaper on this basis back in 1985, the *Weekly Mail* (now the *Mail & Guardian*). We said at the time that the media were focused on the institutions of dying white power, Parliament and the Union Buildings, rather than the emerging structures of new political power in the townships and on the factory floors. The future was being shaped not just by those who occupied the halls of power, but those who were knocking on the door and demanding entry. To understand the future, you needed good old shoe-leather reporting, which would tell you what was happening on the ground in communities around the country.

Again, some 25 years later, we are in danger of immersing ourselves in the admittedly entertaining shenanigans of power involving big men and the occasional big woman in the same halls of power, and not paying enough attention to those important – but barely visible – elements of our society who do not have access to those halls and are gathering outside in large and voluble numbers.

The period 2008–10 saw a wave of xenophobic attacks and what were called service delivery protests, but coverage was limited largely to journalists parachuting in to the location, grabbing a few hurried interviews, accepting what was said at face value and presenting the pat explanation for what was going on. The authorities were dismissing these events as either straight criminal activity or the result of a conspiracy; others accepted the premise that people were frustrated with the slowness of government delivery on their election promises – all of which were patently insufficient explanations for these outbursts of violent frustration. The pictures were dramatic, but the reporting told us little about why it was happening at that time, why it was happening in some places and not others, or who was involved in it. Since this was a serious threat to the country's stability, and a direct challenge to the ANC's transformation model, it was frustrating that it did not get more in-depth attention.

This is partly because, in the 'rainbow nation' spirit of reconciliation, and in the determination to make a young democracy work, most of us did not want to face up to the most threatening and difficult issue in our society: the vast gaps in wealth and access to jobs, services and opportunities. Driving on the road running north from Johannesburg, it is tempting to avert one's eyes and drive on. But nothing is more likely to disrupt this country's stability and prosperity than the fact that a large section of our society is gaining little benefit and watching others enjoy it disproportionately.

These thoughts were nascent in my mind when in mid-2010 I had a conversation with Chris Vick, a former colleague who was now special adviser to the Minister of Human Settlements, Tokyo Sexwale. Chris had managed Sexwale's high-profile visit to Diepsloot in 2009 and he told me of the cauldron of political intrigue and factionalism which he had to swim in to arrange the visit. It struck me immediately that this vital political dynamic was not being reported, that journalists had missed this in explaining the visit and we were largely oblivious to the substantive implications. I set out to learn more about it.

Diepsloot has much to offer as a microcosm of the country's political and social dynamics at the cutting edge of service delivery issues. It includes some of the most deprived areas of Joburg, and it sits alongside conspicuous wealth. It is a post-apartheid settlement, which is unusual. It is volatile, having seen at least six outbreaks of violent protest in the last two years. It has been a centre of xenophobic attacks. It hosts the ANC's branch of the year for 2009. It has seen some development, but not enough. And it is accessible.

Learning about a place like Diepsloot turned out to be like measuring a coastline. If you look at a small map, then the coastline usually looks quite simple and you can measure it with relative ease. Pick up a more detailed map and the shoreline gets more jagged, is more complicated to measure and each twist and turn makes it longer. The closer up you get, the more twists and turns there are, and the longer it gets. This is, of course, what scientists call fractal theory, the study of shapes which can be split into smaller shapes, each an approximate reduced-size copy of the whole. The French-American mathematician Benoit Mandelbrot first coined the word 'fractal' when trying to measure the coast of Britain. Measure it with a centimetre-rule and it will be much longer than if you used a metre-rule, which would be longer than if you used a kilometre-rule. The length is determined by how you measure it as much as by the reality of the coast itself.

Each time I visited Diepsloot, I saw some nuance, some new detail which disrupted the pattern I thought I had seen the day before. Each interview opened up new complexity and as I probed that, it led to further detail. Each time I thought I recognised a community, I realised it broke up into smaller communities. Each time I found a pattern, I quickly found disruptions in the pattern. The closer I looked, the more detail I found, the more complex it became. But a journalist's job is to find the patterns, to make the complex understandable, to take outsiders in without confusing or bewildering them, to achieve the apparent contradiction of revealing complexity with simplicity.

Diepsloot is in the throes of a rapid transition from an informal area to full integration into the city of Johannesburg. Its political and social structures grew organically in a situation where there were no rules or regulations, no rule of law, and few state institutions to impose order and structure. So people organised themselves into street committees, which formed community courts, and the Community Policing Forum, which patrolled the streets and dealt with crime – filling the vacuum created by the absence of police and lack of access to the justice system. They made their own rules, enforced by these structures, about who could put up a shack, where they could do it, and what facilities they could use. They set up their own crèches and informal orphanages. The authority of political leaders spread into all sorts of areas in which they would not normally hold sway. As you might expect, the structures were often corrupted and crossed the line into protection rackets. The community courts sometimes behaved like kangaroo courts.

Now the state is trying to impose the structure, order and control which it needs to do what states do, such as provide security and deliver services. It has to clear shacks to allow roads into the area, to be used by police, ambulances or service delivery vehicles; it is trying to number every shack in order to get a hold on who is coming in and where they build a shack, and to try and constrain that growth; it is trying to introduce policing and stop vigilante groups killing suspected criminals; it is trying to impose health and safety rules on the orphanages and crèches which popped up of their own accord; it is bringing in the rapid bus public transport system to try and displace the grip of the taxi industry; it is moving to stop people stealing access to electricity and water; and – as the ruling party – it is trying to introduce its own street committees to displace those used to mobilise protest.

In a democracy, the state can only do this in conjunction with the organic, bottom-up, informal structures, and attempt to co-opt them. So it provides police to go on patrol alongside the Community Policing Forum. It negotiates with the politico-civic organisation Sanco to try and clear road access. It employs members of the community to number shacks and report when new shacks go up. It sets out to establish a formal township and create a township register.

The gradual introduction of policing provides a good example of how state structures work alongside informal ones. When I went out on patrol with the CPF, the police stood back while community volunteers conducted searches, sometimes giving a few sharp blows to those who offered resistance, but taking those who were found with weapons and putting them in a police van waiting nearby. Police could not go at night into many of these areas on their own – they would be outnumbered and outgunned, and the roads are too bad and the area too dark and crowded for them to be safe. But they made it clear that they would not tolerate vigilantism. The CPF, for their part, needed the police for legitimacy, because with the police on their side they can enforce rules, hand over culprits, and avoid getting themselves charged for vigilante action. Besides, if they did not work with the police, there would have to be a clampdown. The CPF and the police have to work together, and patrol together. The police seek to introduce rules, uniforms, order, and the CPF help police get in and catch the bad guys. Now the role of the CPF is largely a matter of timing – to get to a crime area when the local community has caught the criminals, give them enough time to teach them a lesson, but not enough time to kill them, and then hand them over to the authorities to take them through due process.

As things go forward, and the new police station is eventually finished and opened, police say they will give the CPF an office and they will become a more regular community forum. The CPF say their job will be to keep an eye on the police and make sure they are doing their job effectively and without corruption. Since many of the CPF people are reservists who want to become police, they have a mutual interest in this absorption. The resistance, though, will come from some members of the community who will lose influence and control and access to the financial opportunities which come with them, when these structures are absorbed by the police.

As you can imagine, the business of numbering shacks in order to impose control over who is there and start a process of allocating housing, is also a contested process. Since there are people who make their living from shack farming, there is going to be disruption. The first time it was done, the machine that produced the bar-coded identification was stolen and someone was selling numbers, so the system broke down and had to be restarted. Spend time in the area and you can still see shacks going up every day.

In the long run, the state structures are too strong and powerful not to take control, but we have learnt elsewhere that it is not easy to stop the theft of electricity, to move people in shacks particularly if they have been moved before, to control the taxi industry, and to regularise pre-school education if you are not able to offer sufficient resources to improve it.

And then there is the unfinished police station, the clinics that close at night, the shipping container classrooms, the mess of roads, the 70 per cent of residents who do not have proper shelter ... If the state is to establish its presence, it has to deliver the necessary structures, institutions and resources – the normal elements of civic and communal urban life – to make the area work, to displace those who fill these gaps with their own structures and authority. That is never easy in a densely populated informal settlement, and it is much harder in one that is politically fractious and volatile. If I have learnt anything in the time I have spent in Diepsloot, it is how complicated and difficult is the challenge the place presents to the city, the province and the central government. It will take enormous skill, will and resources to tackle it.

Add to this the fact that Diepsloot is one of 182 such settlements competing for attention and money around Joburg, and 1 700 around the country – each of them potential sources of volatility and violence if they are neglected, every single one a visible reminder of the harsh inequalities inherited from our past, a deep scar upon the urban landscape. You get a sense of the scale of the challenge.

Like the Giant African Bullfrog, Diepsloot is an indicator. When the water and air are good, the Frog will come out in Diepsloot East and fornicate and eat, and you will hear its bovine 'mooooo'. You will know there is an environmental problem when The Frog falls silent. With Diepsloot, it is the opposite: you will know there is a problem when it is volatile and noisy. But it is as certain a sign of the state of health of this city, province and country.

There has been abundant rain in this area in the summer of 2010/11, causing floods in some parts. The Frog has had three or four breeding opportunities as a result and has been procreating profusely. Stand in the marshy fields on the right evening at the right time of year, and you will hear its cry.

At the moment, all is well with The Frog.

Now listen for the sounds coming from Diepsloot.

ACKNOWLEDGEMENTS

Over a period of months, I have interviewed hundreds of people in Diepsloot, and experts who have done work there. I cannot possibly mention or thank all who gave me of their time and knowledge, but I can say that I was received with heart-warming openness and generosity, for which I am very grateful.

Apart from those quoted in the book, there were many who went out of their way to assist. This includes the office of Executive Mayor Amos Masondo, Inneke de Villers-Engelbrecht of Johannesburg's Department of Development Planning and Facilitation and the Corporate Geo-Informatics Department. Professor Dave Everatt, Chris Wray and Graeme Gotz at the Gauteng City-Region Observatory helped with research data.

Yamkela Khoza translated lyrics for me and journalism students Slindile Nyathikazi, Malcolm Rees, Kiral Lalla and Uviwe Mangweni assisted me with research and interviews. Thanks also to Michael Nkosi and Diep Movement for allowing me to quote lyrics.

Phillip Makwetla and Chris Vondo were two of those from Diepsloot who gave me invaluable guidance and assistance. If Phillip tires of politics, he has a future in journalism.

Wits University gave me the space and time of a sabbatical to do the work, and the Reuters Institute for the Study of

Journalism hosted me in the congenial writing atmosphere of Oxford University, with the help of the Anderson Capelli and Oppenheimer funds. Thanks to the Wits Dean of Humanities, Professor Tawana Kupe, for his support.

Editor Ivan Vladislavic's impeccable advice, always delivered with grace, assisted my difficult transformation from a newshound who could produce 800 words in a hurry to someone who might be able to structure a 70 000-word narrative. Editor Frances Perryer knocked it patiently into shape, line-by-line, with great care and understanding. Publishers Jonathan Ball and Jeremy Boraine must be thanked for their enthusiasm for the project from day one, as well as Francine Blum and her production team of Michiel Botha and Kevin Shenton for a sterling job of design. Thanks also to the generous and hugely talented Alon Skuy for an excellent set of pictures of Diepsloot.

The quote on Page 4 of the Epilogue from Wits's Forced Migration Studies Project is taken from *May 2008 Violence against Foreign Nationals in South Africa: Understanding Causes and Evaluating Responses,* by Jean-Pierre Misago, Tamlyn Monson and Loren Laundau (Forced Migration Studies Programme, 2010)

The 1996 Social Survey quoted on Page 13 in Chapter 1 was done by Setplan and quoted in *Land Use Management and Democratic Governance in the City of Johannesburg, Case Study: Diepsloot* by Rebecca Himlin, Hermine Engel and Malachia Mothoho (PlanAct).

I have also drawn on the Community Agency for Social Enquiry's valuable research, *A Quality of Life Survey in Low-Income Areas in the city of Johannesburg* (Case, 2006).

For those who want to know more about frogs, Vincent Carruthers has written a number of books. His most recent is *A Complete Guide to the Frogs of Southern Africa,* written with Louis du Preez (Random House/Struik, 2009).

In writing about xenophobia, I have drawn on *South Africa's*

Xenophobic Eruption by Jonny Steinberg (Institute for Security Studies, 2008), *May 2008 Violence against Foreign Nationals in South Africa. Understanding Causes and Evaluating Responses* by Jean Pierre Misago, Tamlyn Monson, Tara Polzer and Loren Landau (Cormsa and Forced Migration Studies Programme, 2010) and *Immigrants in Johannesburg: Numbers and Impacts* (Centre for Development and Enterprise, 2008).

The quotes from Linda Silberman and Tanya Zack can be found in their insightful essay on housing in *Go Home or Die Here*, edited by Shireen Hassim, Tawan Kupe and Eric Worby (WUP, 2008). Also useful have been the writings and displays of Thorsten Deckler and his team at 26'10 South Architects (see www.2610south.co.za)

I also drew on *Land Use Management and Democratic Governance in the City of Johannesburg. Case Study: Kliptown and Diepsloot* by Rebecca Himlin, Hermine Engel and Malachia Mathoho (Planact). For some of the earlier history and developments, I drew on *The Rise and Fall of the 'Community'? Post-Apartheid Housing Policy in Diepsloot, Johannesburg* by Claire Benit (Urban Forum).

Orapeleng 'Geo' Letsholonyane assisted me with Development Bank research and documentation, as well as thoughts and ideas.

I pray I have done justice to the views of these people. For those officials who ducked and dived and declined to talk to me, I hope I have done justice to you as well.

Finally, the biggest thanks are due to those closest to me who have put up with me and my absences during this project: Harriet, who is always my first reader, editor and adviser, Jesse and Georgia, who gave me consistent support and essential encouragement.